SUCK LESS AT GOLF

Jeff Beck

ISBN:1979713154
ISBN-13:9781979713153

For anyone who has ever picked a range, given a read, or scrubbed old mud off of someone else's wedge.
This sport wouldn't exist without you.

About This Book

Hi.

We need to have a quick conversation, but this format doesn't really allow for a back and forth, so instead just pretend that I'm only talking to you and nobody else. You can decide if this book is right for you before you get too far into this. Hopefully you've decided to download the free chapter or you are leafing through a copy before pulling the trigger. No point in wasting your money or time if this isn't the book for you.

You don't know me, but there's a good chance that I know you. Maybe not you specifically, but who you are as a golfer.

If you are contemplating reading this book, you likely fall into one of the following categories.

1. You enjoy the game, but you wish you were not the worst golfer in your usual group. Maybe you feel like your friends resent your presence on the golf course. I'm certain that they don't, but if you are convinced of it,

having a stranger tell you otherwise probably doesn't make you feel any better.

2. You play for a multitude of reasons -- business or networking or nostalgia, pick one -- and you'd like to improve.

3. You play golf regularly, but all too often you attach your mental state of happiness to your performance, which leads to all sorts of fights with your significant other about wasting time and money just to make yourself angry.

4. You are on the cusp of winning the bottom flight of the club championship, and you are willing to do whatever it takes. Except move up to the next flight.

5. Your burgeoning Tour career has fizzled, likely due to too many injuries/caddie/swing coach/swing thought changes, and at this point you're looking for any port in the storm.

6. You hate golf, but you are also a masochist, and the thought of reading a book to learn the finer points of golf puts your skin on edge -- and that's what really gets you off.

7. You received this book as a gift, or for playing in a charity golf tournament.

If you are making a push for the Tour, or Senior

SUCK LESS AT GOLF

Tour, or Mini-Tour, I cannot help you. You will probably read this book and shake your head, thinking that the insight I am giving is equal to telling people that they need to continue breathing in order to live better -- because most of what we're going to cover you already do, and have done, for years without a second thought. Let me assure you, that makes you the outlier. The overwhelming majority of golfers do not do the things that you do. They do not think about the sport the way you do. And hopefully in a few hours, they will.

If you received this book as a gift, and you are wondering if it is worth your time, then ask yourself this question. "Can I shoot 82 or better regularly?" If the answer is yes, then you will probably not find a whole lot in here for you. If the answer is no, you really should keep going.

If you are a golf masochist, well, way to embrace it and lean into your thing, I guess. No judgment here, but damn. If you are so inclined, there's gotta be a local shrink's kids that your advanced therapy regimen could put through college if you wanted a different path.

For the rest of you, this book was written for you. The purpose behind this book is to help the average golfer play better golf without requiring a life change to

Jeff Beck

get there. I've spent more than twenty-five years in and around the golf industry, and at a certain point I started to recognize that there were certain behaviors and patterns that all decent-to-great golfers exhibited. The flip side of that coin is that there are a different set behaviors and patterns that all less-than-decent golfers exhibit.

If you are looking for a book to give you an idea of how to improve your short game by choosing the right type of shot for each circumstance, this might be the book for you. If you are looking for a book to teach you the perfect swing, this isn't it. If you are looking for a statistical analysis of virtually anything, this isn't going to be your jam. I do cite statistics a handful of times, but the vast majority of my advice comes from firsthand knowledge and experience of dealing with literally thousands of golfers and would-be golfers, who all struggled with the same issues that you are.

This book will help you develop a better practice regimen. This book will help you find a good teaching pro, if that's a route you want to explore -- and explain exactly what you should be getting out of *that* relationship. This book will help your course management, both in the way to play better golf, as well as play faster golf. This book will help you put together

4

the best set of clubs for your game, even if it means sacrificing a little misplaced pride. If that sounds ideal -- then this book was written for you.

There isn't one swing that is ideal for every single golfer. Jim Furyk's oddly-shaped swing is evidence of that (check YouTube if you can't picture it), so trying to spread a One Perfect Swing Gospel™ is an exercise in futility. Molding someone's swing takes dozens to hundreds of hours of hands-on instruction. Trying to do so via absentee third party, for example through a book, is the very definition of impossible. I would have better odds starting a cult. And while that would probably be more fun, it wouldn't really help anybody.

This is not a mechanical instruction manual that's going to tell you where your right elbow should be at the top of your swing. If you are looking to stop throwing strokes away by running through your game on autopilot, or just doing what everyone else in your group does -- you are the right reader for this book.

If all of that that hasn't scared you off, then let's jump in. We have got a lot of work to do.

Strengths & Weaknesses or Be Realistic

I hate to break this to you, but you probably think you are better at golf than you really are. It's cool. We all do it. Tour pros do it. They attempt shots with little chance of success, which will oftentimes cost themselves massive sums of money. It wasn't pride that kept them from laying up in front of that lake guarding the green. They overstated their own ability to themselves.

We all do it.

I first encountered this when I started my first job, selling golf clubs. Our store was the first of its kind in Arizona, with more than thirty-five thousand square feet of all things golf. Even though it was called Golfsmith, we still had people wandering in and asking where the tennis equipment was. Seriously.

But, the people who came in for golf clubs and golf club advice were overly ambitious. Part of the summer-long training regimen for salespeople was becoming comfortable with a series of questions that we were to ask any customer that would allow us to penetrate their cloud of delusion.

I know this sounds a little vague, so let me give you an example. Golf clubs have shafts, and those shafts flex a certain amount. In order to find the right club for you, you need to match your flex to your swing speed. The faster you swing, the stiffer the shaft that you need. And that's great and very easy to follow along. But not many people want to admit that they are only a Regular flex. And they certainly don't want to admit that they are a Light flex and absolutely, under no circumstances, would a full-grown man want to admit that he needed a Ladies flex (no matter how slowly he swings).

And that was why we had our training program. Because if the guy that needed a Light flex ended up buying the Stiff flex that he wanted, it was only a matter of time until he came back unhappy. As well-trained employees we had questions that we would ask (and a decent attorney would have called out "Objection, leading the witness!" over most of them) but they told us what we needed to know, and not just what the customers wanted to tell us.

One of the first questions was "How far do you hit your driver?" Can you believe that 99% of everyone that walked into that golf shop (just a few miles from one of the largest retirement communities in the country, Sun City, Arizona) could hit the ball further than all but one golfer on the PGA Tour at the time? Remember hard drinking, hard living, hard hitting John Daly? Yeah, they wouldn't be able to knock it past his absurd ~315 yard average drive, but everyone else on Tour was a chump. Everybody who came into the store hit it 285-290 yards, but they claimed that they were the shortest in their foursome, and that was their story, and they were sticking to it.

I dealt with this type of customer at least five times a day and on the weekends, that number would hit double digits. Everyone poked it just shy of three bills every time they were on the tee box. *Everyone.*

Which is why we had a follow up question, that asked virtually the same thing the opposite way.

"What club do you hit from 150 yards?"

In other words, you've hit your monster 290-yard drive, and you have 150 left to the stick, what are you going to hit? Oh, a five-iron? Hmm, that's interesting. Because if you were to really hit the ball 290 off of the tee, there's only a couple clubs between a driver and five-iron, and you have 140 yards of leeway there. So, either the customer has a number of very strangely bent clubs (which is illegal, for you folks who champion the USGA and their so called "Rules of Golf"), or they are lying about the distance that they hit it off of the tee.

It wasn't hard for me to run the numbers in my head based on how much golf I had played. At the time, I was a thick 17-year-old who actually could hit it 275 or so off the tee, and my 150 club was a solid eight-iron. I played with guys who played college golf or were the top of their high school teams. They could hit that mythical 295-yard drive that everyone claimed to have in their bag. And their 150-yard club ranged from a smooth nine-iron to a stepped-on pitching wedge.

Side note -- there are all kinds of ways to describe the way a golf ball is hit. I've always gone with "smooth" or "stepped-on" as my goto descriptors. A shot that is hit "smooth" means you hit a shot just a bit soft, taking a little bit of speed off of the swing. "Stepped-on" is like mashing the pedal and it means that you tried to swing extra hard. It might be stupid, but that's how it's always worked in my head.

Anyways, since golf clubs are designed to give you a ten-yard gap between sticks (done by changing the loft of the head and the length of the shaft a precise distance --

it usually checks out regardless of ability), if he really was hitting his five-iron 150 yards, that means his four-iron really goes somewhere in the 160 range, and a well struck three-iron should go about 170 yards. Hybrids hadn't been invented yet, so let's say he was carrying a driver, three-wood, and a five-wood. Stands to reason, his five-wood would go 185 or so, his three-wood would be in the 200 range, and his driver would likely go 220, maybe up to 230 on a good day. These aren't perfect numbers, and I wouldn't want to choose his clubs as his caddie based on this but, they are close enough to get the information we needed standing in that fluorescent-lit store.

Someone who hits their driver a max of 230 yards (not counting massive downhills or wind) should not be hitting a firm or stiff shaft (frequently the same thing, labeled by different companies, though a few companies employed both in their lineup, just further obfuscating the landscape) and should certainly be a Regular flex. Then it was a matter of finding a way to break the disappointing news to the customer, which could be tough, especially if they were thinking of buying a new club. It was a little easier if they already had the club in question, and just wanted to change shafts for a variety of reasons.

Meanwhile, a couple shaft makers had gotten wise to

this predicament, and developed a line of shafts that had a different naming system. So a Ladies flex in everyone else's club was now a Regular, a Light flex in someone else's club would be labeled a Stiff for them, and the Regular flex for everyone else was suddenly an Extra-Stiff. We sold a bunch of those, the customer got what they wanted and needed and no man had to play with a Ladies shaft.

Because I was a 17-year-old kid at his first job, I wasn't able to tell the customer the hard truth that they didn't want to hear (from a 17-year-old kid of all people), but here you are reading my book, so I can tell you the truth. You can take it.

You need to acknowledge the truth of your game.

You need to see through the mental gymnastics you put yourself through, and you need to be brutally honest about your strengths and weakness.

You need to see through the cloud of illusion you've created around your game, because the only way to improve it is to be completely honest with what you are starting with.

You have to know where you are starting, in order to figure out where you want to finish. And where you want to finish is the most important part of this whole process.

Jeff Beck

The guy who wants to shave five-to-ten strokes off of his game is on a different journey than the guy who wants to overhaul his swing (and his life) and in eight years make a bonafide attempt to make the Senior Tour. Neither one of them is wrong, but they both have to figure out where they are today in order to figure out where they are going and how to get there.

You cannot keep lying to yourself, if you legitimately want to change your game.

Okay, so that was harder than I thought it would be. I came across like a life coach. I'm not your life coach. I'm just the guy who's going to make you better at golf.

The whole point behind addressing your weaknesses is so that you can plan around them. Golf is a unique sport. It's one of the few where, even in a competitive venue, the other guy's performance doesn't really affect your abilities. This isn't basketball, where they can keep double teaming your best player. This isn't football, where their all-pro nose tackle is locking down your passing lanes over the middle. This isn't even marathon running, where the top runner in the world is pushing pace for the first ten miles, hoping to wear you out.

This is golf. Where the only person who can affect you is you. Sure, if you are playing Match Play and your opponent is already in for par, you need to make par or you've lost the hole. But even if you do lose a hole, they don't get to remove a club from your bag. They don't get to stand in your way. They won't (unless they are a monster or a sociopath) talk in your backswing. They can't stop you from hitting whatever shot you want to hit. They have to stand there and watch, as you impose your will on the course.

Which means that you have to learn which ways the course will win, and which ways you will win. Here's the most basic philosophy of course management: You need to figure out what your favorite club is. Not the one you spent the most money on, or has the best head cover, or looks the coolest. I mean the one that you know you can always hit. The one that is your bread and butter. *Your* club. We're not doing street magic, so it doesn't matter if you tell me what it is or not, but start thinking about what you think it is. That club is going to be the easiest way to improve your game.

Since no one can force you to play the game a certain way, you get to make the decisions on the golf course. Which means you should spend your time on the course not painting yourself into a corner, and instead leverage your newly acknowledged strength as often as possible.

If your seven-iron is your go-to club, your new goal is try to play every hole to that distance. For argument's sake, let's say that your seven-iron goes 165 yards. Now you are going to get very good at subtracting 165 from different lengths, and that's your new shot. If that means not hitting driver on the short par-4 that's only 330 yards, so be it. Quick math says, that at 330 you can hit your seven-iron off of the tee to give you a seven-iron into the green, and if you've really been grooving your seven-iron, then neither shot should have any drama and you should be somewhere on the green, with a putt for birdie.

In this example, you could try the other way, and hit your driver off the tee. 330 is a weird length, because the odds of you getting all the way there are really low. But it's short enough, you're probably going to step on your driver and try to get there, and now the odds of your shot going poorly just skyrocketed. However, let's say that you can restrain yourself, you don't swing for the fences, and you just try to hit a normal drive. Realistically you'll usually end up with an okay tee shot. Which means you've hit it 275 yards (which tracks with a seven-iron that goes 165, your real numbers will vary) and you now have 55 yards left to the stick.

I don't have a 55-yard shot, and neither do you.

SUCK LESS AT GOLF

Nobody does -- it's a dead zone. You have a 55-yard partial shot. A half swing. A tweener (as in "in betweener" -- yup, it's a stupid word). An awkward shot/ swing that, more often than not isn't going to end up very well. And certainly not as well as your trusty seven-iron that you've grown so fond of.

But, you went through the normal motions, and you grabbed your driver to hit from the tee, and hit your okay drive. Then you followed that with your tweener second shot, so now you aren't even on the green. But the version of you who went seven-iron/seven-iron has a twelve footer for birdie, so all those disparaging remarks you made about him hitting a seven-iron off the tee are making you look even more like an ass.

It becomes a little trickier, and the math isn't as clean, if your sand wedge is your go-to club. Partly because it doesn't have enough length to be useful that often, but, much like we don't choose who we fall in love with, we don't choose what club feels like home for us. That said, if your go-to club is a wedge, *and* (and that's a big *and*) you can put the ball where you want most of the time, then all is not lost.

It seems counterintuitive, but you will likely be better off playing everything to 110 yards (for argument's sake, we're going to say your go-to club is a 52-degree gap wedge which sits in the large gap between a 48-degree pitching wedge and a 56-degree sand wedge -- hence its clever name) instead of just dealing with whatever hand the golf course gives you.

Let me explain:

In this exercise, you only hit it 250 with a driver. Your five-iron goes about 170, which means your eight-iron should go about 140, which places your gap wedge around 110. We're also going to assume that you hit half of your shots your normal length, and the other half a little less (with the exception of your go-to club, the gap wedge, which you hit spot on 80-90% of the time). Your longer clubs you hit well less often, because the truth is, most golfers don't hit their long irons and fairway woods nearly as consistently as they do their mid-to-short irons.

The first hole is a 420-yard par-four. You pulled your driver out of bag, hit it well, which left you a five-iron to the flag. You missed your approach shot by just a little, not too terribly, but enough that you missed the green, and you didn't get up and down. You just made a bogey five.

If you were to replay the same hole again, the odds would be good that the drive would be less than ideal (since the driver is hard to hit and like most golfers you are inconsistent), leaving you more like a three-iron into the flag. But three-irons are even harder to hit well than five-irons are, and you miss that too. Bogey is the name of the game, and double-bogey probably comes into play more often than par does because short games can be finicky. If there's a green side bunker (which I just added to this fake hole) then it further compounds the issues.

Instead of running this scenario over and over, where you make bogey 60% of the time, double bogey 25% of the time, and par 15% of the time, take a step back, and leave the driver in the bag.

Hitting a six-iron off the tee (which should take any drama out of the first shot) will leave you with 260 to the flag. Then you grab your seven-iron, swing smoothly, and aim for the middle of the fairway (if you haven't noticed, most fairways are exponentially wider than most greens -- hitting a fairway with a mid-iron should be a pretty easy most of the time), which should leave you with your magic number of 110 yards. At that point, you grab your gap wedge, hit it at the stick, and see how it works out.

Regardless of your putting ability, you should make par far more than 15% of the time -- especially if the gap wedge really is your go-to club, so you aren't taking 40-

foot putts. 10-foot putts are far, far easier to make, but you can't expect to make them all.

The biggest difference in this situation (besides making more pars) is how many fewer double-bogeys you will make. If you are standing in the middle of a fairway, holding your favorite club, you should be hitting the green more often than not.

The biggest way to drop scores is to eliminate the blow-up holes. You aren't trying to break the course record or shoot even par. You are trying to play better golf. If better golf means a bogey every time (which should result in a score of 90 or so, depending on your local track's par), then so be it. Bogey golf is nothing to sneeze at if you've been struggling to break 100.

If you don't have the confidence to stand at 110 yards, hold your gap wedge and know in your heart that your next shot will likely be a putt, then you have some work ahead of you. You need to spend a lot more time with that club, and only that club, getting it ironed out. That one club is going to be your best method to lowering your scores, so you need to understand the subtle nuances of how you and it interact.

I would strongly implore you to warm to a club with a little more length, however, like a six-iron (160 yards), seven-iron (150 yards), or eight-iron (140 yards). That will give you a lot more flexibility when playing your game. If one of your wedges is giving you the siren call, maybe spend an afternoon with your seven-iron, and see if you can't break the spell. It will pay off in the long run, giving you an extra 30-50 yards to play with each hole.

And that's nothing to sneeze at.

What's Worth Working On

The last chapter gave you a glimpse into what course management is, how to figure out what your strengths and weaknesses are, and how you can use them to your advantage. Now we're going to cover some universal truths.

There is no argument or debate to be had. It is a fact, that the players on the PGA Tour are the best golfers in the world. The 156 guys who tee it up each week are on a different level than anyone else. The things that they can do with a golf ball are unparalleled. Sure, there are long-drive competitors and trick shot guys who can do some insane stuff, but as the whole package, the guys on the Tour are the best.

You should not attempt to emulate them. Instead, you should look at the second-best group of golfers in the world.

The ladies of the LPGA Tour.

The leg up that the ladies hold over the men, is that

they play much smarter. They play the numbers far better than the guys. The guys do everything they can to overpower the course, and make the course bow to their whim.

If a hole is a dogleg right with a massive tree that can block the second shot? They just swing extra hard, bomb it over the corner and now that tree isn't an issue.

And that's great -- if you can pull it off. The reality is that there are a few hundred people on the planet who truly *can* pull it off with any regularity, and I can assure you, neither of us is one of them.

I've been to a number of PGA Tour events. Every one of those guys *is* the one who could pull it off. It's like that line from the movie *The Social Network*.

"You know how you'd know if you invented Facebook? You'd have invented Facebook."

If you had the ability to overwhelm a golf course, you'd be doing it, right now. It isn't some latent mutant ability that's going to show up when you walk into an enchanted sand trap somewhere. The guys who can overpower a golf course have been doing it for years, and they've worked their asses off to do so.

If this comes off like sour grapes, it isn't. I'm just trying to hammer home that few people get to big-foot a course. The rest of us need to use tricks and cleverness to bring the Goliath down. And the ladies on the LPGA Tour do that every week.

We're going to channel those old Choose Your Own Adventure books for a second.

A. Have you ever stopped a golf ball with spin?

B. Have you ever backed up a golf ball with spin?

C. Have you never put enough backspin on a ball to influence its path?

If A, then great.

If B, then great.

If C, then great.

Unless you are the type of player who puts an insane amount of spin on the ball, with every iron, even your long irons, then you shouldn't plan on it happening. Relying on backspin to stop a ball on the green is like walking a tight rope. That's life as a Tour Pro. The rest of us don't bother, but those guys know they can do it -- blindfolded.

If you can't reliably stop a golf ball with backspin, you have to find another way. Luckily, it isn't rocket science as much as it is landing the ball short, and allowing it to run.

Allow me one of what will be many tangents in this

book.

At my first Member-Employee tournament (I was apparently well liked by the golf shop staff that decided the teams) I was paired with a member named Roe McBurnett.

Picture your favorite grandfather. Picture his favorite person. That's a poor imitation of Roe McBurnett. He was the liveliest, late-70's to early-80's person I've ever known, and what's more, he knew it. He always had a joke, but was quicker to smile at your response. I cannot tell you how many times he shot his own age or better. As far I know, he always did.

And he was my playing partner for the day in a two-man scramble.

Keep in mind, he couldn't hit it out of his shadow, and we were playing the tougher of the two courses. I figured we wouldn't finish very well, but we would have an enjoyable morning, and that would be that.

We took second place, with very little input from me.

Over the years, Roe had figured out how to play the course instead of getting slapped around by it. Instead of putting extra effort into his swing, his swing was always in control. He put the ball exactly where he wanted to and just made his way through the round, with little to no fanfare. Watching Roe play close up was boring as hell but a pleasure to watch.

If the stick was in the middle of the green, without fail, he'd land his shot at the front of the green and let it run back, resulting in a five to ten-foot putt. If the pin was in the back of the green, he'd land his ball in the middle of the green, let it run back, resulting in a five to ten-foot long putt. If the pin was up front on the green, he'd land it short of the green, run it back, resulting in a five to ten-foot long putt.

We had, and made, a lot of five to ten-foot putts that day.

Meanwhile, I was doing everything I could to show him how well I could strike the ball. I aimed right at every pin and, every now and then, I'd be on target. Of course, when that would happen, something would arise that I didn't see (like a big left-to-right slope in the green, that Roe would incorporate by aiming a little further left). More often than not, I didn't hit it just right and my ball would end up running another twenty feet past the pin.

He never chastised me for it. The last place in the world to give someone advice, especially your own playing partner, is on the course. You show up with the game you brought and you need to play with it. But as I put my eight-iron back in the bag, he'd grab his five-iron, take a smooth and buttery swing, and leave the two of us with a five-foot putt for birdie.

It happened all day long for Roe, and it happens all day long for the LPGA Tour.

Which is exactly why you should start emulating them.

Be aware of your surroundings and what the course is throwing at you. Look at the pin. Where is it, what's blocking you from it, and what's the green going to do when you land the ball up there. A positive outlook doesn't hurt any.

If there's a green-side bunker left, maybe don't aim at the pin on the left side of the green. Aim to the right of the green, knowing that if you miss it a little, you will only be in the rough, instead of a bunker. Or, if your sand game regularly works, go right at the stick at the pin. Growing up in Phoenix, I played a number of courses that all but gave up on golf course maintenance in the summertime, due to the heat. As a result, I got to play amazing courses for pennies on the dollar, but I also got to play courses that had sand that resembled one large patch of dirt-colored cement. It was so dry and hard, it didn't flake at all. You could run a ball right through it and it would ramp up onto the green.

Running a ball through a bunker and ramping it up to the green is good work if you can get it, but I wouldn't count on it with any regularity. All it takes to fool this plan is for a suddenly zealous member of the grounds crew to run a rake through the bunker and it would return to its soft, punitive state.

Back to the point -- the ladies of the LPGA Tour don't try to overpower a golf course, they are more than happy simply outthinking it. And that's something anyone can learn if they want to, and what's more, that's the type of thing that can stick with you for the rest of your life.

If you rely on your physical prowess to overpower a course, that will only last as long as you are on your game. Look at Tiger. From 1997 to 2013, he was one of the top five ranked golfers every year but one, and he was ranked number one almost every one of those years. In 2014, he was 17th, 2015 he was 321st, 2016 he was unranked, and as of this writing in March of 2017, he's the 757th ranked player in the world.

As they say on the internet, 1) that escalated quickly, and 2) life comes at you pretty fast. He had a number of off-course *ahem* distractions take him away from the game, but the biggest change was that he simply got old. He knew it was coming -- the man spent his twenties revamping his swing repeatedly in order to make it less taxing on his back. But the reality is, you cannot swing that hard that often and not have long-term repercussions.

Meanwhile, Roe McBurnett was playing better golf at 80 than he was at 70. His physical game hadn't changed a whole lot, but he had 10 more years to understand the courses he regularly played. By not relying on perfection, things never went poorly for him. Margin of error is *everything* in golf, and you'll come to find that out -- if you don't know it already.

If you've played more than a few rounds, you already have your own collection of stories, where shots *almost* went perfectly for you. That chip shot that hit the pin and bounced away. That putt that rode the lip, started to fall in but the momentum took it out of the cup. The drive that landed middle of the fairway, hit something (maybe a sprinkler) and kicked hard right into the rough instead of kicking forward and down the slope for a free fifty yards. Keep playing. You'll eventually have so many *almost perfect* stories that you'll forget about them, because you'll have enough *actually perfect* stories to overwrite them. But you need to stack the deck in your favor.

I had a boss once who had a saying. "You can set yourself up to win or you can set yourself up to lose." It sounds trite on the surface, but there's some deeper wisdom there. Much like people deriding John Madden for saying "I think the team that scores more points is going to win this game," you can get reductive and turn up your nose at the football guru, or realize that he's saying it's going to be an offensive slugfest, with very little defense being played by either side.

So set yourself up to win. Your ego might take a hit, by hitting a lot of irons from tee boxes, and your playing partners may make comments (or at the very least throw some strange looks your direction). At the end of the round, however, your scores will be lower than they would have been if you'd just mindlessly grabbed your driver every time, leaving yourself a collection of half-wedges and bad lies.

Don't worry, you'll still get to hit plenty of drivers. Unless the course is designed to cut off your fairway early, you're automatically hitting driver every par 5, and there will be a number of par 4's that will work out for you natively. Going back to the same numbers from last chapter, if your 150-yard seven-iron is your go-to club, then any hole about 400 yards sets up perfectly for you. You'll find there is a certain distance that merits some internal debate, where you'll want to quickly weigh the pros and cons while your partners are hitting, and then carry out your plan.

For example: a 450-yard par four.

You can go driver, for 250 yards, leaving you 200 in, provided you hit your tee shot well. That should put you in five-wood territory, and only you can say if that's a good thing or not. Personally I've gone through stretches where I had actual confidence in my fairway woods to hit the ball exactly where I wanted them to with any semblance of accuracy. Those stretches have been rare and short-lived. Historically, my irons fueled my game and I've carried fairway woods as a better method to hit it a little shorter off the tee, or simply to advance the ball in a general direction on a par-5, provided I don't care that much about the next shot's lie.

Remember that shot Corey Pavin hit in the 1994 US Open? The one where he blasted a four-wood to a few feet to seal the deal? Yeah, that has never been me.

But in this scenario, you are playing and not me, and you have a little confidence in your five-wood. Let's say you end up in the basic vicinity of the green, pin high, just a bit right, plugged in the bunker (five-woods tend to hit the ball high. A ball landing in the sand from a very high height has a propensity to dig deep into the sand). It takes you two swings to get out of the sand, leaving you twenty feet for bogey.

More than likely, that means you are going to make double bogey.

Then there's the other way play the 450-yard par four. Consider it the path less traveled.

There's a number of options to turn two swings into 300 yards, which will put you at 150 yards to the pin. You could take your five-wood off the tee (200 yards), then follow it up with a sand wedge (100 yards), before hitting your seven-iron in. But, that would probably be less than ideal -- unless your seven-iron is *dialed* in, you'd be better off reversing that, and hitting your sand wedge into the green. Very few people are more accurate at 150 than they are 100, provided that your 100 yard club is still a full swing. So, let's say you hit five-wood, followed by seven-iron, leaving a full sand wedge in.

Again, the second way may not yield many more pars, but it should reduce the number of double bogeys you make. This is setting yourself up to win. Eighteen holes is a long stretch. You aren't going to win every hole, and you get to define what "winning" a hole means. A 450-yard par four is the course's knockout punch, and counting on making bogey every time you play the hole isn't admitting defeat, as much as you spotting the course a freebie. Let's be honest, if it was only a little longer, say in the 470-485 range, then the hole would probably be bumped up to a par five, and you'd get that stroke back.

As it stands, you can play the hole for bogey, and unless you have a full-on breakdown or malfunction of some sort, that should be the end of it. It's a lot better than double-bogey, and a world better than triple-bogey -- which frequently show up as a result of trying too hard for par. Take your bogey and move on.

While a difficult course may have a knockout punch, you don't have one. There's no single act on a golf course that can let you win. Making a hole-in-one is great, but there's seventeen other holes that are opportunities to give those strokes back. And that's why you can't win the game of golf on one hole, but with a big enough blow-up, you can lose a game on one hole.

Starting out with a ten on the first hole has effectively ruined the day before it got started. That will permeate your decisions for the rest of the day -- which is why playing smart is so important. We are incredibly bad at actual risk versus reward analysis on the golf course, and frequently risk everything in order to gain a slight advantage.

If you can make different shot choices to limit your exposure on the course, you will ultimately shoot better scores without changing a single part of your swing or improving your short game. That said, when your short game improves, that's when the big changes will start happening on your scorecard.

About My Background

Before we go too much further, here's a little bit about me. Well, no. The little bit about me is at the back of the book. This is decidedly more about me, so you understand where I'm coming from. If you are willing to grant the premise that I know what I am talking about, and don't feel like reading a mini-biography, the next chapter awaits you.

I started golfing when I was 6. Or rather, I was 6 when I fell in love with golf. My parents had moved us to a newly developed master-planned community in Glendale, Arizona, and our house backed up to the 12th green to the country club. I'd spend hours standing on our back fence, just watching bad players putt, and I was captivated.

Eventually I started hopping the fence to putt whenever I thought the last group had come through, dodging the ranger who came around to pick up the sticks at night. A few times I got caught flat footed only to realize that the grownup in the golf cart didn't seem to care all that much that I was out there since I wasn't being an asshole and doing anything malicious to the green.

Fast forward a few decades and I now realize that the guy picking up the sticks is the lowest man on a big totem pole. Unless I was pouring gasoline all over the green and flinging lit matches at the puddle, he probably wasn't going to say a thing. He had bigger things to worry about. Live and learn. Kids are stupid.

I golfed very poorly throughout my childhood, and got a big eye opener in high school at the golf team tryouts my freshman year.

I was bad. Like, didn't make it past the first two days level of bad. The coach said I showed promise, which probably spoke more about how nice he was or related to me being a pretty good student in his class. I showed many things, promise wasn't any of them, but Coach didn't need to rub salt in any wounds.

What that meant is that when I hit 16, I was unencumbered by the obligation to represent my school on the golf course, and I could get an actual job to go along with my extracurricular gig as the sports editor of the high school paper.

SUCK LESS AT GOLF

Eventually one of the largest golf-only retail stores in the country opened up a few miles from my home, and I got a job as a sales associate. A couple months of rigorous training while the store was getting put together meant that we spent a lot of time drilling the questions we were to ask folks in order to ascertain what they really *wanted*, and what they really *needed*. In real estate there's a phrase "buyers are liars" and it means that most clients will tell you "We can't buy a two story home, we need at least four bedrooms, and maybe we'd like a pool" but in the end they mean "We want a pool more than we care about the number of bedrooms, and if the pool is good enough, we'll buy a two-story home in a heartbeat." It happens every day with home buyers, so you can imagine how commonplace it is among golfers debating a new set of irons.

I sold golf clubs for three years until I left for Northern Arizona University up in Flagstaff. After my freshman year, I moved back down to Phoenix for the summer (not the brightest thing ever to abandon the beautiful pines of Flagstaff for the blistering hot desert) and went back to work in golf retail for one last time before returning to NAU in the fall. The following year, I stayed in town for the summer after getting a job working outside service at Forest Highlands, one of the top golf courses in the country (there are rankings and lists and everything), and that was it for my golf club selling career.

I worked outside service at FH for the rest of college, and was sad to leave the place behind to get a "normal job" out in the "real world."

Six months into the "real world", I found myself back in Flagstaff for a weekend, and met up with some of my old buddies. Several of them had transitioned from outside service into the golf shop as assistant professionals. It sounded like a great job, with a bunch of the guys I'd worked with, and loved working with for years. And they needed one more, they let it be known after more than a couple beers. A week later, I started in the golf shop as the newest assistant professional at Forest Highlands.

The only downfall to the job was its impermanence. When the season ended in a few months, I would need to go find another job because at 7,000 feet of elevation, Flagstaff's golf season is fairly limited. There's a solid four-to-six month period of time that golf is off the table. So after my first season in the golf shop, my DoG (that's Director of Golf to you -- we'll cover golf course hierarchy later) got me a job working outside service down in Scottsdale at Troon North, one of the top public daily fee golf courses. It was kind of a step down since Forest Highlands was literally the top course in the state (regardless of public or private status), but at least it was a job.

What I wasn't anticipating was just how differently everything would be between the courses. Troon North is the flagship course of one of the largest golf management companies in the world, which meant that there was a well-defined corporate structure and this golf club was smack-dab at the top of it. If you worked long enough in outside service, and if you were good enough, you would move into the shop as an assistant pro in their system. If you made assistant professional there, it was only a matter of time until you got an assignment somewhere as a head pro. Somewhere. You wouldn't have a choice in the matter, it could be Idaho, or Ohio, or somewhere else in Phoenix, but you would be a head professional. Compare that with FH, where the relatively new Director of Golf had been working there for the better part of two decades as an assistant and then head professional.

It was a different world. And I don't know if the shift

was because of private versus public, or locally owned versus corporate, or something else, but it was palpable. At the same time, the job duties were somewhat confusing. The outside service staff at Troon North did virtually all of the outside of the shop duties that the assistant professional at most other courses do. At FH, (and later I would learn many, many other courses), one assistant professional would stay inside and man the golf shop, answering the phones, checking groups in, ringing up purchases, that type of thing. The other assistant pros on duty would be outside the shop. Typically one would be responsible for the pace on the course, by way of rangering or marshaling the course, while another pro acted as the starter and kept groups moving to the first tee in a timely manner. Assistant pros are the feet on the ground, keeping an eye on the whole operation to make sure that everything is always running as it should.

At Troon North, assistant pros resemble bank tellers. They stand behind the counter in the shop, rocking a tie, and running credit cards for greens fees all morning long. If the golf shop needed to speak with someone from outside service, they'd holler on the radio and we'd come up the stairs to see what the problem was.

The outside service staff started the first tee, rangered

the course, and then did all the normal outside service stuff too -- cleaned clubs, attended to the range, cleaned carts, manned the bag drop, etc. And that meant that if you worked outside service, you never stopped moving. If you opened, you'd get there an hour or two before sunrise and you'd be ready to call it a day shortly after noon. The closers came in around noon, and they would spend all afternoon holding a wet rag and running bags around to the bag drop where they would wait for the player's inevitable departure. It wasn't rocket science, and it was a well-oiled machine that kept everything moving pretty quickly. Troon North was a public club, with only a few memberships, so almost everyone we saw on a daily basis hadn't been there before, and wanted to take in the cool, but expensive experience. Meanwhile, our job was to keep things moving, because there were a dozen people coming in right behind them. Coming from a club where customer service was priority one, trying to adopt a customer service not-quite-last mentality was a little rough. But I was running around hard enough not to think about it.

Meanwhile, one of my buddies from the shop in FH, Joe, had gotten a job out in Hawaii. It was a private course, and he was caddying, but we'd talk every few weeks and compare notes.

In literally every single way, he won. While Troon North had two very nice courses, and they are among the top courses in the state, Joe's course in Hawaii, Nanea, could be considered among the best in the world. If, you know, they wanted to. That club did everything in their power to stay off of everyone's radar, because they simply weren't equipped to deal with the attention. On a busy day at Troon North, I'd see more than 200 golfers from each course, both of which fed back to the same clubhouse. Nanea thought 28 golfers was a relatively busy day, and 56 golfers was an insane number.

But out there, customer service was truly everything. The membership was a collection of the wealthiest people the planet had to offer, and the club had one general rule. Check your ego at the door and enjoy yourself.

That went for everyone. Members, guests, employees, it didn't matter. If you couldn't relax, have a good time, and treat everyone around you like they mattered just as much as you, they didn't want you there.

I thought Joe was pulling my leg. Every company talks about how "we're a family here", and golf courses are no different, but at the end of the day, it's a flawed

40

comparison unless your family likes to make your cousins feel like second-class citizens. In reality, members are members, employees are employees, and that's the end of it.

At the end of the season, Joe bailed out of the golf world altogether instead of coming back to the golf shop in Flagstaff. However, before he jumped ship he put in a good word for me out in the south Pacific, and the following winter I found myself on a flight to Kona to spend the winter caddying. When I arrived, I learned that yes, in fact, Joe had lied all about Nanea.

It was so much better than what he said.

He'd been downplaying it the whole time, perhaps to spare my feelings. Or maybe I'm just easily impressed -- though literally every person I know who's stepped foot on the course has been blown away by it. The fairways are better than most others courses' greens. Seriously.

The irony was that I'd only caddied a handful of times before getting a job as a caddie. I spent those few rounds trying to remember and embody the caddie credo: Show up. Keep up. Shut up.

That's what golfers expect from their caddie. Or hope to expect from their caddie. The universal bar for caddie greatness is set pretty low, which could be a reflection on caddies throughout history.

Not in Hawaii, however. We weren't lugging bags around as much as we were on course concierges. The course is incredibly difficult, and as a result, every group had to take a caddie with them. One of us would ride on the back of the cart, giving yardage and club advice, and reading putts for each of our players, then hustling over to replace divots, rake bunkers, or put clubs back in the bag.

The job was more about anticipating needs and taking care of something before your players could ask you to. You never stopped moving if you were doing the job right. If I hadn't spent nearly every afternoon in one of the several oceanside bars with my co-workers, I would've dropped forty pounds.

The course was carved out of volcanic rock, they literally had to build a foundry to crack through the centuries old dried lava to get to the soil, so the aesthetic was unique. The fairway led to the rough, which eventually led to black rock punctuated with "fountain grass," tall weeds that kind of resembled willows that when the wind blew somewhat resembled the sound of running water -- hence the clever name.

The wind made the course more difficult. There were

very few trees on the course, and the layout was no slouch either -- but the main reason for the difficulty was the greens. Nanea was built on the side of a dormant volcano, so your horizon was somewhat skewed. As a result, a putt would look and feel flat, but in reality would break toward the ocean. Everything always broke toward the ocean. You could have an uphill putt, or at least it'd look uphill, but if it was toward the ocean, you'd have to treat it level, or even downhill.

Frequently our assertion of what a putt would do was questioned -- and rightfully so. If you've golfed more than never, you know that a ball doesn't break uphill, so players would assume we were giving our read the wrong way. The caddie trick was to tell them "it's the grain", as in the grain of the grass was special and going to treat the ball differently for some mystical reason, but in hindsight I don't think that was accurate. However, it's far easier to tell someone "the grain" will move the ball instead of "No, there's more break than it appears because we're on the side of a mountain," over and over again.

That first season flew by in the span of a long afternoon, and I returned to the golf shop in Flagstaff for another go around at my cushy assistant professional job. After getting used to running around a course, reading putts and giving club advice, standing on a driving range with a clipboard, telling the 8:20 group that they were next on the tee, and asking one of the outside guys to carry Mr. So-and-So's bag back to his cart, felt a little hollow. When I returned for my second season in Hawaii, I stayed the entire year, working through the summer and playing as much golf as humanly possible. As an assistant professional I had great playing and practice privileges in Flagstaff, but in Hawaii, even as a caddie, I had even more opportunities to play. And at the end of the day -- it was Hawaii. Not a terrible place to spin your wheels for a few years.

As great of a life as it was, I knew it wasn't one that I wanted forever. And I had enough co-workers who were deep in their forties and fifties to know that if I didn't leave soon, I never would. After three seasons, I hung it up and left the industry all together. While I was fortunate enough to work at some of the best courses in the country and around the world, my fondest memories are of the people I worked with. The men and women I worked with were phenomenal people, and golfers, and living in their world was eye opening. Before I worked in the industry, I knew guys who claimed that they were scratch golfers, and make no mistake, they were good.

But after playing with legitimate scratch golfers on a regular basis, the difference became very clear.

My time in golf was spent standing on the shoulders of giants. I worked with dozens of men who won accolades for their abilities as golf professionals (which is similar but ultimately very different than professional golfers). And while I gave more than a few lessons, everywhere I looked, I was surrounded by guys who had devoted their lives to the game. Many of the points in this book come from my conversations with them, as much as my own experiences on and off the course. All of this contributes to the reason why this book is filled with insight and cerebral exercises instead of swing tips or on range drills. If you can conquer the six inches or so that occupy the space between your ears, you've done the hardest part. Then you'll just need to learn to trust yourself.

Finding the Right Pro

The hierarchy in the golf industry is more complicated than most people realize. Everyone thinks that the head pro is the top of the food chain, and there are a few assistant pros under the head, and that's it. At one point in time, that was probably true, but it isn't any longer. At least, not at most golf courses.

More often than not, the real head of the operation is the Director of Golf. He or she oversees the whole operation. The head pro (and depending on facilities, you may even have two or three head pros) answers to the DoG. From there you may have a First Assistant, followed by a number of Assistant Professionals, and then perhaps different Merchandising Associates -- but Merchandising Associates are typically relegated to staying inside the golf shop and wouldn't be qualified to give you a golf lesson.

Many courses also employ a Director of Instruction, but those typically don't answer to the DoG, at least on a daily basis. They kind of run their own thing, and usually stay out of everyone's way, just kicking ass on the range and making golfers better. In my experience, if you earn the title of Director of Instruction, you not only know your way around the range, but you also know your way around the membership. I've never seen a membership not *love* their Director of Instruction, even if they don't all go to him or her for lessons.

The reason I'm telling you all of this, is because most people's response to the idea of getting lessons, is to march into the golf shop and ask for the best teacher they have. And with almost zero exceptions, that would be the Director of Instruction. But that's probably not who you actually should take lessons from.

I'm not saying this to take money out of their pocket. There are plenty of people who should be speaking only with the Director of Instruction. But if you are struggling to break 100 or 90, then there are more people on staff who can help you achieve your goals, at a far lower cost per lesson.

The Director of Instruction, and DoG's hourly rate as well, is going to be the highest at any facility. After that, you'll have the Head Pro, then the First Assistant (if your course has one), and the least expensive will be one of the Assistant Professionals. And I'll never argue that an Assistant Pro is as well versed as a DoG or Director of Instruction, but for most golfers, the differences won't be noticeable. Not to say that the Directors would teach over your head, as much as the subtle nuances that separate a good instructor from a great one will be lost.

That said, I don't know your budget. I don't know if you cringe at a $400 driver, or decide to plunk down the cash and order two when you heard that the Tour-spec version is only $750. It's not my place to spend your money for you. I would say that you should spend up to what you feel comfortable with, but you absolutely shouldn't get a second mortgage to pay for lessons (though I am a huge advocate of taking lessons from professionals). That also doesn't mean listening to your buddy, who has a half-dozen golf magazine subscriptions and reads them cover to cover. Find a pro. A real one, with certifications and everything.

Once you've established what level of professional you want to work with, you need to spend time speaking with them. Is there chemistry? You aren't looking for a date (unless you are but that's not covered in *this* book) but you should be able to have a conversation with the pro.

SUCK LESS AT GOLF

Does he or she make you feel uncomfortable when you ask questions?

Does he or she actually listen to what you want to improve? Or do they keep pushing the conversation over to something else?

Does he or she map out how frequently you are going to come back for more lessons? Unless you are doing a full swing reconstruction, a laid-out series of lessons is probably overkill and a good way to ensure that the pro has a steady stream of extra income. When I was at Nanea, I became good friends with Jason Bangild, the Head Professional there and one of the nicest people you will ever meet. I mean, he's Canadian, so to begin with, he's already about 90% of the way there. One of the few things that gets him visibly angry (the Maple Leafs playing bad hockey being another one) was seeing an instructor map out a schedule of lessons with a client over the next month or two. Jason started every lesson with the phrase "I hope I never see you again. At least, in this context," or something similar. He had confidence that if you spent an hour with him, he should be able to fix whatever needed fixing. He's not wrong. If you want a follow-up lesson, ideally weeks or even months later, so be it. Get a touch-up.

The hardest part of the process, which is where the biggest improvements will come from, is taking whatever they just taught you and applying it to your game on your own. The pro isn't going to follow you around for the rest of your life, and remind you that you shouldn't lock out your back knee as you get to the top of your swing. He isn't going to use the grip end of a golf club and force your knee forward every time you do it. You need to do that for yourself, *after* the lesson.

Most pros I know will check in on you weeks later. And it wouldn't be uncommon, if they were to see you warming up for a round, to discretely watch what you were doing -- and look to see if you were putting what they taught you into practice. If you were, they'd tell you. If you weren't, a good pro wouldn't say anything about it. Hearing that you are screwing something up is the last thing you need to hear as you are warming up for a round. Good golf pros know that.

Bad golf pros want to teach you the same thing over and over. Doing that can buy them a new Mercedes and you will likely not improve in any discernible measure. But that's okay, it's only been seven months. "These things take time."

I had the opportunity to work adjacent to Hank

SUCK LESS AT GOLF

Gardner, who was the Director of Instruction at Forest Highlands for most of the time I was there. You're not going to find a better guy than Hank, and he definitely wasn't the type to get a client on a repeat track. I watched him firsthand politely tell members that they weren't allowed to come back to him for another lesson until they'd spent more time working on what they'd already worked on. But that's because Hank knew he was good. I've seen Hank "fix" so many golfers with just a few words, that if this was a few hundred years earlier he'd need to avoid the greater Salem area at all costs. He's a no-bullshit pro, the kind of guy who doesn't overcomplicate anything, in an industry that tries to overcomplicate everything.

For example -- and this is the closest thing to swing advice that I'm going to give at any part of this book -- here's how to improve your chipping.

BLT.

B. Put the ball BACK in your stance. So if you are right-handed, the ball should line up inside your right foot.

L. LEAN toward the target. That puts more weight on your front foot, which is your left foot if you are right-handed.

T. TILT the club toward your target. That de-lofts the club some.

Then you do a putting motion and that's all a chip shot is. Putting the ball back in your stance, and leaning toward your target gives you a much better chance to hit the ball crisply, and not chunking it into the ground.

Hank didn't complicate any more than that. He stuck with BLT and explained what you needed to do to make it work. Literally everybody in the short game clinic got it in the first minute or two, and started chipping measurably better immediately.

What I haven't told you, is that this was a junior clinic that Hank was running. There wasn't a golfer over the age of 12. 7-year-olds picked up what he was putting down but I've watched him give the same lesson to executives. Everybody gets BLT, and everyone walks away better at chipping.

There are good golf pros and bad golf pros. If your vision of a golf pro lines up with Carl Weathers, half-heartedly watching his clients over a magazine as Adam Sandler blasts 500-yard bombs down range, that's largely inaccurate. Hell, that's inaccurate for bad pros. That's a full-on neglectful pro, and those generally don't exist in the real world. There are enough people who want to work in this industry that that kind of attitude would find someone unemployed pretty quickly.

But back to your search for the right person. When you've figured out what level of pro you are looking for (based on how much you'd like to spend) and you've found someone that you get along with, it's time to figure out exactly what you want out of the relationship.

This isn't a marriage. This isn't even a long-distance semi-casual dating thing. This is the exchange of goods and services and you need to show up already knowing what you want to know.

I've had clients show up for a lesson with the mindset "I want to get better."

That doesn't help. Nobody knows your game like you do and it's up to you to figure out what needs work. Remember at the beginning of the book when I said you frequently needed to be honest with yourself? This is one of those times.

Take a good, hard look at your game. Not your scorecard, your game. Picture the last round that you played. Where did the double bogeys happen? Any triples? What caused those?

Here's what (literally) thousands of hours, on and around golf courses, have taught me is the most likely way it went down. Unless you actually put it out of bounds (OB) and had to walk back to the tee box hitting three, it wasn't your tee shot. The same thing with your second shot. Sure, it would have been nice if your approach did not land in the bunker, giving you with a terrible lie, but it is what it is. Leaving it in the sand for your third shot, then blasting it over the green for your fourth stroke didn't help. And yes, if your fifth shot -- a pitch shot that probably should have been a chip shot -- had ended up closer to the stick, that would have been nice (everybody is better at four-foot putts than they are at twenty-four-foot putts). If we're going to go ahead and wish for things, we might as well wish for the bladed-out sand shot that was the fourth shot to have gone right into the hole and stopped the problem as it began. As it was, the first putt hit the back of the cup and popped out, leaving you a tap-in for a triple-bogey seven.

In that description, virtually every facet of your game could be improved, which is normal. There's never been a golfer that thought "Yup, I'm happy with where my game is." Good putters wished they were great putters, great putters wished they were amazing. Until you shoot an 18 for a full round, there's always room for improvement (fun fact: it'll never happen outside of a video game, but it's a good carrot to dangle in front of yourself). In the meantime, we still need to figure out what part is the most worthwhile to improve.

In the previous scenario, the putting wasn't bad. Any time you can two-putt from twenty-four feet, be happy with that. Be very happy with that. Not to say that you shouldn't give it some attention in the future, but it's far from your most pressing matter.

Your off-the-green short game -- including chipping, pitching, flop shots, green side bunker shots and more -- counted for three of the seven strokes you took. I wasn't a math major, but I'm pretty sure that's nearly half of your strokes. There's an argument to be made that, if your approach shot was better, then the "Catastrophe in the 12th Bunker" (that's what your friends are calling what you just did) never would have happened. However, that's some backward logic that I'll address next chapter. For now, just go with me.

Simple logic says that 3/7 strokes (sand, sand, pitch) makes it your most egregious weakness, and that's where you should start. Which means, that's what you tell your pro that you want to work on. Where the pro goes from there is up to him or her. I have my methods, everyone else has their methods, and I'm the last person to get between a golfer and their pro. I just want to help you get your message across in order to get what you need. The short game is complicated enough, and has enough facets, that it wouldn't be insane for that to cover more than one lesson. It all depends on how fast you pick it up. The chip is very different from the pitch and the sand shot is completely different from everything else. But on their own, none of them are very hard to pull off. The hardest part is figuring out what type of shot you should use, once you have all the different shots in your repertoire.

Why the Short Game Matters

In the last chapter, I said it was backward logic to think of working on your approach shot in order to compensate for a weak short game, and that's true. The only place it *isn't* is in a four-player scramble.

If you aren't familiar, a scramble is a type of format, where everyone hits a tee shot. Then as a group you pick the best one, and everyone hits their next shot from there. For some reason, among amateur golfers, it is frequently called "best ball" but it isn't. A "best ball" is where everyone plays their own ball for the entire hole, and only the best score on the team counts. Scrambles are largely more fun for casual rounds and a great approach shot is key to making a great score in a scramble (having four chances at an eight-foot putt gives you a good chance at making it, but four runs at a thirty-foot putt will still usually end in a missed putt). However, I'm not going to advocate you model your game to excel in scrambles.

I want to make you a better a golfer, or at the very

least, I want to help you *suck less. At golf.*

The reason that you don't want to bolster your approach shots, in order to compensate for deficiencies in your short game, is because of the failure rate. Much like baseball (where failing six out of ten times throughout your career *will* land you in the Hall of Fame), golf is a game based on screwing up. That goes for every level, even the best who've ever played.

Tangent time. Hang on tight.

When I worked in the shop at FH, I had aspirations to become a head professional one day. Which meant that I needed to get my PGA Class A certification. There's not a golf course in the country that would hire me as a head pro without it. The PGA program takes several years, has three levels that include book work to demonstrate your knowledge of the industry, followed by a testing phase in Florida that lasts several days. Once you've tested out, you ascend to the next level and do it all over again.

To get started in the program, you need to pass the PAT, which is the Player Ability Test. They need to make sure you can play some pretty good golf in order to work in the business. The PAT is a one-day event where you play two rounds, and the cut off is fifteen strokes over the rating. They try to make things easy by putting the pin in the middle of the green -- or at least in the flattest area of the green -- and you play from the white tees. Usually a par-72 course will be rated 68ish to 70ish. So double the rating, on average, would be 138 to 140, add 15, and you have a total of 153 to 155. Meaning, you need go out and shoot a couple rounds somewhere in the mid-to-high 70s, or better.

Again, they are trying to make things easy by picking relatively easy courses with easy pin placements. Only about twenty percent of the field passes each time and so much of that is the mental side of it. Having the pressure of "if I don't pass I can't start the program" weighs on golfers. I've met players at the PAT who looked like junkies, they were so nervous -- one guy had failed nine times and if he failed the tenth time his course was going to let him go. Yikes.

While you aren't technically competing against anyone else in the field, in a sense it is tournament golf. I've been told that "the difference between casual golf and tournament golf is the difference between badminton and weightlifting."

I would agree with that sentiment.

I crashed and burned hard during my first PAT attempt. It was ugly. But after, having one under my belt gave me a better understanding of what was to come. I scheduled another about a month later and made my game my top priority. One afternoon, I was banging balls on the range for a solid two-hour stint, when one of our members strolled up and asked what I was doing. I told him I was getting my game together for my PAT and he shook his head at me.

The member in question -- lets call him Dave -- was a former PGA Tour player. He'd had to retire from golf early, due to a degenerative muscle disease. It had robbed him of the ability to hit the ball over 220, but his mind was still there. And hell, the guy had played in the same group as Jack Nicklaus half a dozen times. If the man told me that north was really west, I'd probably have listened.

Dave looked at me, pointedly, then my bag, then the driver in my hand, then my bag, and back at me. It was like he was doing a bit on stage.

"PAT is 15 over the rating, right?"

Dude hadn't played competitive golf in decades, and he never joined the PGA (the PGA and the PGA Tour are two separate entities) and yet he knew exactly what I was looking at.

I nodded.

"So what the hell are you hitting so many drivers for?" he asked.

"I had a number of bad breaks on tee shots during my last PAT."

He shrugged. "Who cares. You need to get on to the green and that's it."

I must have looked at him incredulously, because he kind of exhaled and launched into it.

"Listen, best player in the world still misses, what, six greens a round? Maybe seven? And you aren't him, but let's say you still hit half of all greens. I'll give you benefit of the doubt and say you two-putt every one of them. Or at least you make a birdie for every three-putt. Right away, half the holes are pars right there. But for the other half, you're going to need to get up and down as often as possible. If you miss half of all greens, and you get up and down half the time, that means you should only shoot nine over. That should pass you, no problem."

To understand what he was saying: the best players on Tour will usually only hit twelve to fourteen greens in regulation. That means that they hit the green with their first shot on par-threes, with their second shot on par-fours, and with their third shot on par-fives. It's frequently better than that for the guys leading the tournament, but if you look at the overall numbers for the year, it checks out.

More importantly, I'm not one of the best players on the planet, so I'm going to miss a whole lot more greens than that. Knowing that pin locations were going to be easy, and that I was a pretty decent putter, he was giving me the benefit of the doubt of getting a two-putt whenever I was on the green.

The big question mark was getting up and down on a regular basis. Up and down is when you are off the green and you spend one stroke getting up (onto the green) and the second stroke getting down (into the cup). Getting up and down effectively means that you saved par on a hole where you missed the green in regulation.

I'd only been golfing twenty years at that point, and I'd never thought of golf like *that*. The ability to hit shots isn't the only thing that separates great players from the rest of us. The space between their ears is a big part of it too.

Anyway, Dave was right. No matter how good you are with the full swing, you are going to miss a lot of greens. If your short game is dialed in -- and I mean *dialed* in -- you should be able to get up and down quite frequently. The element that too many golfers miss, is that a series of pars is as good as a string of birdies and bogeys that come from living dangerously and charging at every opportunity.

Play for par, and set yourself up to make the easiest par you can.

Instead of hoping against all reason that you'll always hit the perfect drive and the perfect approach shot, and hit the perfect birdie putt (but at the very least you'll tap in for par) you need to be realistic about what is actually going to happen on the course.

Some drives will be good. Some drives will be amazing. Some drives will bring shame to your family, they are so bad. The same goes for every shot. Well, let's hope that none of your putts commit war crimes, but I think you know where I'm going.

The short game is your way to cheat the system. A good short game can cover virtually any deficiency. If you can get the ball within thirty to fifty yards of the green, your short game can take over.

Much like TYPING IN CAPS LOCK CAN BE CRUISE CONTROL FOR AWESOME, having a killer short game can be cruise control for lower scores. I mean, it isn't really cruise control because you still have to work at it and think about it, but in time, you can develop the touch to hit the shots that you want, as well as the knowledge of when to hit which type of shot.

There are effectively three different types of short game shots and each one is unique.

The first, which will likely be the staple of your short game, is the chip shot. Yup, BLT from the last chapter. A chip shot comes off the club face low, carries a short distance, and rolls exponentially more than it was in the air. A typical chip shot should be in the air for 10-20 percent of the total length of the shot, and roll on the green for 80-90 percent of the length of the shot. You can use damn near any club to pull off a chip shot, but most commonly, you'll use a pitching wedge, sand wedge, or gap wedge; those all give a good height on the initial pop to get over and through whatever stands between you and the green.

But you can try stuff out. Get weird with it. See what works for you. For example, there are more than a few Tour Pros that have used fairway woods or hybrids to pull off an exceptionally tricky chip from super deep rough (because those club heads have a tendency to not get caught up in the thick grass like a wedge) and that was a smart play. Furthermore, with enough time you can develop enough feel to let you purposely chip the ball into the rough surrounding the green. The heavy grass will help you out and take most of the speed off the ball and then the remaining inertia will carry the ball forward on the green. The hard part is figuring out how hard to hit it and where to land the ball, so that there is enough momentum to escape the rough and continue trickling toward the hole. I can't tell you the number of times I got cute with it, chipped to the edge of the rough, only to have the ball stay there and force me to chip again on the next shot.

When in doubt, play the numbers and make the smarter play. The exceptions prove the rule; you are better off putting than chipping, pitching, flopping, or anything else. Before you argue, consider this: most players get frustrated when they leave a putt five feet short, but would be elated if they chipped to five feet. This is all the evidence that you need to prove that putting is more accurate. Regardless, your best play is to get reliably onto the green every time, and if you can aim closer to the stick without increasing the likelihood of mistakes -- then do so.

When hitting a chip shot, you need to read the green closely, because your ball is going to go with the break once it's on the ground. That can be good or bad, but either way you will need to address it.

Again, the chip shot is executed by a modified putting stroke. Just remember BLT. Ball back in your stance, lean toward the target, tilt the club head forward. De-lofting the club (by tilting it forward) helps keep you from popping the ball up -- which is good because when a ball is popped up into the air it doesn't have a tendency to run once it hits the ground.

The second shot you need to have in your repertoire is the pitch shot. It's not a polar opposite of the chip shot (that would be the flop shot), but it is in the ballpark. A chip shot has a 10-20 fly and 80-90 run ratio, the pitch shot is more 30-80 fly and 20-70 run. The wide range is due to how much more versatile the pitch shot is, since a pitch is effectively a partial swing. The pitch is also far more complicated, since you still need to figure out where you want the ball to land and where you want the ball to stop moving. There are two schools of thought on how to accomplish this.

One way to go is to think of any club in your bag as a potential to pitch with. Each club will have its own individual shot characteristics. Sure, you can use a seven-iron to pitch the ball 35 yards, but there's a good chance that if you land it on a normal-sized green, it will run off of the back. Whereas if you had grabbed your nine-iron, that extra loft may have stopped the ball from running through the back of the green. This is a good opportunity to harness your inner Roe McBurnett and figure out how far each club runs when you use it to pitch.

Or you can go the other direction. Make a single club, say your pitching wedge (the name is a pure coincidence, I can assure you) and adjust your swing to make each shot happen.

I tend to favor the latter method, which is probably the wrong way to do it, but it's always been easier to wrap my brain around. Otherwise, I have to keep something of a mental database of how far my five-iron runs from various yardage, all the way to a lob wedge. While I can remember a lot of things, that's probably not a good usage of the limited storage I have up top. Instead, I grab my gap wedge and go from there. I tend favor the gap wedge over the pitching wedge, since the extra loft means the ball will go just a little higher, and if I want a low running shot, I would just chip it. Standing over my ball, I'll take a few practice swings, and emulate what I think it will take to get the ball to do what I want.

That's a copout, I know. I've been hitting that shot for

years, but there are certain things that I can't transfer to you via the written word. Touch and feel are two of those. You have to learn and develop those for yourself, and I would *strongly* advise that you do. If you take one thing away from this book, let it be that spending an hour at the short game green is never time wasted. The subtle nuance of what "just a little bit extra" means is different to everyone. Whatever it is to anyone else on the planet shouldn't matter to you. This isn't a pissing contest. It's golf.

The next short game shot you want in your bag is the green side bunker shot. This is one of the least understood shots in the game and most people make it far too hard.

The purpose of the bunker shot is to get the ball out. That's it. Low expectations and, if you get near the stick, fantastic. That'll come with time. Meanwhile, goal number one is just get out of the sand.

Where the shot is commonly misunderstood is the uncertainty between how much sand you should hit versus trying to pick it clean and hitting no sand. Here's the deal. Don't pick it clean. If it's a fairway bunker, and you're a buck-forty out, then yes, try to pick it clean. But this is about green side bunkers.

SUCK LESS AT GOLF

Here's where I break my rule and give some swing advice again. However, it's only because the sand shot is so clear cut, there really is only one piece of advice for everyone.

When you set up to the ball, open your stance. That means that your left foot (for right-handed golfers) is back a few inches from where it normally is. If you could put a yardstick down, pointing at the target, a normal stance would have your toes touching it. With an open stance, if the yardstick were to still touch toes on both of your feet it would be pointing to the left, perhaps by as much as 45 degrees.

Make sure the ball is forward in your stance, kind of like you are hitting a driver or three-wood.

Next you want to dig in to the sand. Really, like a little kid, moving your feet back and forth to plant your feet. You are doing this for two reasons. The first one, without damaging your moral fortitude, is to get a good base. You are going to be making nearly a full swing on loose sand and, if your foot slips, I can guarantee you that isn't going to make things better. So sink into it.

However, there's a rule in golf that says you can't test the sand for consistency. You can't run your club through it, to see how it's going to react. In fact, touching the sand at all with your club, on a practice swing or for any other reason, is a penalty stroke, so don't do it. But if you are digging your feet in for stability purposes and just happen to realize, "Hey, this sand is super fluffy," then so be it.

The next thing you want to do is open up your sand wedge (and it really does need to be your sand wedge -- it is uniquely qualified to let you hit this shot). Opening your wedge means laying it clockwise some, and regripping it. Don't try to just hold your wrists in a certain way to achieve this. That doesn't work. You must change how you are holding the club. Open the club face roughly the same amount you opened your stance. This is what is going to let you hit the ball straight forward and not the roughly 45 degrees to the left of the target, where you technically are aiming right now.

When you start the swing (remember that it needs to be hovering over the sand and not touching it unless you like throwing strokes away) you want to take the club outside of the normal club path. You don't want to take it straight back, because your forward swing is going to be what's considered "outside in." This means that as you hit the ball, you are slightly swiping across the ball from right to left.

The best way to picture this is on the range, or

somewhere that you can swing freely. Take a long iron and set it down, aiming toward your target. Without a ball in play, hover your club over the long iron and think of the line of the shaft as the target line -- if you are directly over it, you are straight back and through. If you start out inside the line, you are influencing an inside-out swing, and if you are outside of the line, that is an outside-in swing. For a full swing, you want to be either slightly in or slightly out. For a sand shot, you want to be deliberately outside the line -- that will encourage your forward swing to work properly.

When you start your forward swing (and this is where the sand shot gets funky) you are not trying to hit the ball. You are trying to hit the sand a little behind the ball. Maybe a quarter inch, maybe a full inch, it all depends on the sand. The reason the club need to be your sand wedge and not something else, is the shape of the club's sole. It has an exaggerated bounce (the added shape to bottom of the sole) which no other club has. That bounce will clear the sand away and pop the ball out. With some practice you can get a feel for how far behind the ball you need to hit the sand. The important part is that you are making a full swing, and that you are following through. If you don't swing through the ball, the club head will simply dig into the sand, and only a small bit of the force you are creating will be applied to the ball. There's always a chance that you will luck your way out of the sand, but more often than not, your next swing will still be from the bunker. Always follow through on sand shots. Then grab the rake and try to make it look like you were never there. If you can't rake a bunker in less than ten or fifteen seconds, you need to practice your raking. I'm not kidding.

The last green side shot that exists is the flop shot, and I'm strongly against you trying it. For one, it has an incredibly low usage rate. Also, it requires an awkward swing, so you would need to practice a decent amount to pull it off. Lastly, it has a razor thin margin of error, and when it goes wrong, it goes so very wrong.

But here we go anyway. Don't tell your mom I told you this.

A flop shot is 95 percent fly and 5 percent run. Maybe even more, like 98 fly to 2 run. Here's how it goes down. The flop shot is kind of like a sand shot, but from the grass. You are going to grab your lob wedge (which has 60 or more degrees of loft) and you are going to open up your stance, and the club face. You are going to start your swing outside, because again, you want to swipe across the ball when you come through. Only this time there's no sand aiding in the experience. You have to slip the club under the ball, so it goes very high in the air. This is what leads to its abrupt stop.

Here's the problem (well, problems) with the flop, because there are more than one of them.

1. You have to take a full swing and you are likely no more than twenty yards away from the stick. If anything goes wrong, and you blade it ("blade it" is the term for hitting the ball with the leading edge of the club), you just hit the ball at least 70 or 80 yards. You consciously took a twenty-yard shot, added a stroke, and gave yourself a sixty-yard shot. It's the golf equivalent of paying someone twenty bucks to punch you in the ear. Don't do it.

2. In nearly every scenario where a flop shot would be ideal, a pitch shot would be almost as good with far less risk. If you need to carry the ball over the rough, or a bunker, or a cart path, and then stop, that's exactly what the pitch shot does. Sure, the pitch has a thinner margin of error than a chip shot, but so does walking down the street. A chip shot is literally an exaggerated putting stroke. You mess that up and you are telegraphing to the world that you could mess up a glass of water. You are

the person who trips over nothing. A pitch shot isn't that much more difficult than *that* and doesn't require superhuman timing.

3. If you hit more than a few flop shots a year, you're just showing off. Phil Mickelson is the master of the flop shot. Truly, there's no one on the planet like him, but he's also got one of the best and most inventive short games ever. The dude has literally hit a flop shot, on purpose, so then it ended up going backwards.

He faced away from the hole, and made a swing.

In a tournament.

Seriously.

Don't emulate him. Celebrate him all you like, but that's not who you model your game after -- unless you are just as good as he is. It's like deciding that you're going to play basketball just like Wilt Chamberlain did. Even if you're five-foot ten-inches. So much of what made Wilt into *Wilt* was his size, and his relative size. He dominated the league because he was damn good and he towered over everyone. You can't ignore that little side note. That's Phil and his short game. If you have his talent, then by all means, flop it up. Otherwise, you are spending hours, and likely dozens to hundreds of hours practicing a shot that you'll get to actually use less than ten times between each presidential election. Does that seem like a good use of your time?

If you were to direct all of your flop-related obsession, energy, and practice toward your pitch shot, your pitch game could be top notch. And it's hard to shoot in the 90's if your pitch game is working. Hell, you could frequently break 80 if you could pitch the ball where you want to. Up and down becomes the order of the day.

Think about Dave's example, for a par-72 eighteen hole round of golf. Say you hit only six greens in regulation and none turned into a birdie or a bogey. If you were to get up and down on just half of the greens that you missed then you just shot yourself a little 78 to hang your hat on.

There's literally nothing else you can do to your golf game that will singlehandedly change the way you approach it than dramatically improving your short game. Your confidence will rise, because you start looking forward to getting near the green. That's where the magic happens. We've all hit towering drives, and sauntered off the tee box like a badass.

Admit it, you have. It's cool, I've done it too. And then what happened? Did you make birdie? Eagle? Oh?

Bogey? Double bogey? *Triple bogey?!* Yeah, because you didn't put the time in on your short game. With a well-oiled machine of a short game, bad drives matter less. And they also occur fewer and further between. Let me explain.

Confidence transcends ability. That means that while your short game is on fire, other parts of your game will improve because you feel better about them. You don't care about missing the fairway because the next shot (be it from the fairway or the rough) is still going to put you in pitching distance. At that point, your short game shows up, knocks it to five-to-eight feet and you make the putt.

Because the other thing you've been doing, besides fine tuning your pitches and chips, is getting your putts dialed in.

Right?

Oh. Right, we haven't gotten there yet. That's the next chapter.

Putting

Raise your hand if you've had to take a putt that was less than an inch.

Or more likely, raise your hand if you've ever taken "a gimme" and knocked the ball away from the hole, counting the stroke as good, from an inch or so?

If you've played more than a few holes of golf, your hand should probably be up. That's a stroke poorly used. That half-inch shot cost you every bit as much as it does to hit your driver. It's the oldest cliché in golf, and every group has that asshole that likes to throw around *that* quote. "Drive for show, putt for dough."

If you are the guy that says it to your group, whenever possible, then I didn't mean asshole. I meant source of knowledge and wisdom. Just remember to get extra smug in order to say it right though. Settle down, I'm joking. Mostly.

The bummer is, it's actually really good advice. Not the dough part, 99 percent of us are never going to make any money on the golf course (your $3 Nassau doesn't count, Jerry). I'm talking about the point that putting is more important that driving.

That said, I favor the off-the-green short game as more important than putting, and I'm going to show you why.

These statistics are accurate as of April 1st, 2017, and while they certainly have changed since, each of these general points hold up when compared against earlier seasons' statistics.

Do you recall Geoff Ogilvy? He won a US Open and three World Golf Championships? Damn good golfer, right? Sure, and through 28 rounds this year, he's made 21 percent of his ten-foot putts. He's had fourteen putts, he's made three.

Two-time Masters winner Bubba Watson? Through 28 rounds, he's made eight percent of his ten-foot putts. Thirteen attempts, he's only made one.

Phil Mickelson? In 33 rounds, he's made half of his ten-foot putts. That's eighteen attempts with nine makes.

Jordan Spieth, one of the top golfers in the game, has played 27 rounds this year. He's made almost 59% of his ten footers. Seventeen attempts, and he's made ten.

SUCK LESS AT GOLF

How many Major victories do you have under your belt? I personally don't have any. I've yet to even play in one, let alone make a cut or even finish in the top ten. Is there any chance that these guys don't work on their putting? They do, regularly, and probably more than any amateur works on any facet of his or her game.

And it shows. Because from five feet, Ogilvy has made 87 percent of his putts. Out of thirty-one attempts, he's made twenty-seven.

Bubba's made 82 percent of his five-footers, with eighteen makes out of twenty-two attempts.

Phil's made 78 percent of five-foot putts. Twenty-five makes in thirty-two attempts.

Jordan make 76 percent of his five-footers, nineteen makes in twenty-five attempts.

Making a ten-foot putt ain't easy for anyone. With practice and ability, five-footers can become nearly automatic. Which is why I prefer to tout the short game off of the green. It is far easier to chip the ball to five feet (instead of ten feet) than to plan on defying all logic and reason and just make as many ten-foot putts as you would five-foot putts.

I'd like to make sure you aren't reading that as "I don't need to ever worry about putting," because that's called

<u>Missing The Point</u>. Don't neglect your putting abilities and let them stagnate, but you should set your expectations fairly low. You cannot address a ten-foot putt and be certain that you will make it. You can hope to make it. You can hypnotize yourself into thinking it will happen, but I can assure you, that will mean you are frequently disappointed. No, you should continue to spend time on the putting green. And you should probably spend more time on the putting green than you are right now.

All that being said, just putting a lot isn't going to make you a great putter. The mechanics of the putt are very simple, but the complications that go into *making* putts aren't nearly so simple.

First, some basics on putting. These may be redundant to some of you, but these concepts are foreign to many golfers. I've had this conversation on or around the course a few hundred times.

Every putt is straight, you just have to choose where the straight point is. For example, a ten-foot putt that is going to move roughly three inches from right to left, would be considered "two balls right." This is because you probably want to aim roughly two ball widths to the right of the cup and let the slope do the rest of the work.

80

SUCK LESS AT GOLF

Most reads are in units of cups or balls, because they are on the green already and you can easily envision their size. Telling someone a putt is going to break four-nineteenths of the width of a Volkswagen isn't all that helpful. Even if it's true.

Next putting truth. The harder you hit a putt, the less it will break. The softer you hit a putt, the more it will break. The ball will do what the slope is doing, unless you hit it hard enough.

Hitting it *hard* is not usually the best idea, however. Putting is like the distillation of all things golf, into a single action. Hitting it far isn't necessarily ideal. Hitting it right, or hitting it well, is. That may sound backward, because who doesn't like hitting it far? But tell that to the guy whose seven-iron normally goes 160, and, jacked on adrenaline, hits one 190 and sails the green by thirty yards. Long isn't the same thing as good.

A hole is 4.25" wide and a ball has a diameter of 1.68". That means that you have room for some error but not much. The more excess speed your ball carries when it gets to the hole, the smaller that the hole effectively is. For decades, there's been a philosophy. "Never up, never in," which is the fun and folksy way of saying "100% of the putts you leave short don't go in."

The flip side of that is 100% of the putts you hit long don't go in either. Just hit it the right distance already. Which is a fun, seven-word sentence but it doesn't help you actually make putts. That's okay. If your philosophy is screwed from the get-go (i.e., never up, never in), then you are in for a lifetime of burning the inside edge. Don't ever consciously hit it harder than you think you should. It's a bad habit to get into.

Playing golf is a conscious decision. Nobody wakes up one morning at the first teebox and thinks "Well, I'm here, might as well play." You made the choice to play golf, likely at least a day or two ahead of time. Have the presence of mind to take in all of the information available to you, then make the decision on how you are going to hit your putt.

Putting theory was a common debate over beers when I was a caddie. Everyone had an opinion and a few of the older caddies thought you should ram every putt home. However, most of the guys preferred to envision every putt just dying into the hole. If somehow the hole moved back an extra couple of inches, your putt would end up short. Doing so gives you the biggest effective cup. If any part of your ball touches the hole, you've likely made the putt, since there's no inertia to interfere with gravity. Making a putt is much more satisfying than burning the edge, or even hitting the back lip and popping up in the air (which tells you that you had the right line, just hit it too hard, and now you've got a four-footer coming back, Hercules), and if you had simply hit the putt softer you probably would have made the putt.

There was one member in Hawaii (let's call him Ted) who liked to bicker about every read any caddie gave him. He didn't like being told what the putt would do, he liked to read it himself, and then ask his caddie to confirm his read or correct it. That's not to say we knew absolutely every putt, but after a couple years, you knew what *most* putts would do. It's moving right to left, maybe a ball, maybe two and, depending on how your guy hits it, either of those could be right. Heck, both of them could be right. This isn't heart surgery, you've got some flexibility.

One day I'm caddying for Ted, and he tells me he thinks a fifteen-foot putt is going to break at least three cups, maybe four. I shook my head, and told him no, probably a ball, maybe two balls. At the very most, one cup.

On the course, you know what that means in relative terms, but since we can take the time and break down numbers, that means I'm saying the putt is going to break at least 1.68", could be as much as 3.36", or at very most it's moving 4.25". This isn't a crazy range for a putt to move.

You'd have thought I told him that sometimes the Devil and God swapped houses for a week.

"How the hell could it be either of those? Or both? Do you even know this putt?" He was livid.

I explained, "It all depends on how hard you're going to hit it. If you hit it firm, it's only going to break a ball, maybe ball and a half. If you hit it softly, it'll break a cup."

That didn't help matters. "Well, how the hell do I know how the hell hard I'm going to hit it?" was something he actually said. Out loud. With his mouth. Ted was many things, a poet was not one of them.

"Ted," I said, very calmly. "If you don't know how the hell hard you are going to hit it, then how the hell do I know how the hell hard you're going to hit?"

He missed that putt by a country mile and spent the rest of the round bitching about everything I did. After the eighteenth hole, he slammed the brakes on the cart, and stormed off into the golf shop. I figured that was that; I was about to never caddie for Ted again. It wasn't my aim to anger him in any way. After all I enjoyed the work, but I wasn't going to lose sleep that night.

84

SUCK LESS AT GOLF

A minute later the general manager came out to talk to me.

"Pards," Jim Saunders, the GM said -- Jim called everyone he got along with 'Pards' -- "I don't know what you did, but you just made a fan for life out of Ted."

"What?!?"

"He's in there singing your praises, and that you're the best damn caddie we have."

From then on, at almost every opportunity, Ted requested me to caddie for him. There was talk that the rest of the caddies wanted to throw a parade for taking Ted off their hands. Eventually he learned to trust my reads but he still rammed more than a few putts well past the hole each round. Old habits die hard.

Now as far as reading a green, there are a number of methods. Some people plum-bob, which is where you loosely hold your putter by the shaft with your thumb and forefinger, and hold it up to your face, to give yourself an artificial level -- if the cup or green is very slightly sloping, that should help.

Most people don't know how to read a plum-bob, but they see others do it so they do it too. Here's a solid tip: if you don't know how to plum-bob, you shouldn't plum-bob. It's a waste of your time.

Jeff Beck

Too many golfers look at their putt but not the entire green that they are standing on, and that's a big mistake. When you look at a green, ignore the stick altogether. Pretend that there's no hole in it at all and that can help you get a better sense of what a putt will do. If a whole quadrant of the green slopes down and to the left and your putt happens to pass through that quadrant, guess what's going to happen? There's no magical path for your ball to travel that will betray the overall logic of the green -- you need to look at the big picture.

Rarely, courses will have some sort of feature that can dictate things beyond logic. Nanea is far from the only course where all things moved to the ocean. I've heard of a few courses in central Phoenix that were built around the base of different mountain ranges that run through the city -- and that everything will break away from them. But you can't count on a course providing you with a cheat sheet.

The biggest thing to work on is the pace of your putt. If you misread a twenty-five-foot putt (you think it's going to break three cups left but it ends up three cups right) that's a big whiff. But, if you got the speed right, then you should only have a two to three-foot putt coming back.

86

SUCK LESS AT GOLF

Meanwhile, if you nailed that twenty-five-footer's read perfectly, but thought it was uphill and it was really downhill, you likely have eight-to-ten-feet coming back.

I wasn't a math major, but I'd always prefer a two to three-footer to save par, bogey, or double over an eight-to-ten foot putt for the same score.

What makes this difficult, is that all greens are different. Now, most greens on a given course are going to be about the same speed. The practice green should be very close to them as well. A good maintenance crew will usually give the putting green just as much care as any of the greens on the course, so it does accurately reflect the greens on the course. However, many courses will also have a practice green that you can chip and pitch to -- and you can't count on that green to be as well maintained. The maintenance staff only has so much time in the day, and getting the putting green *right* is more important than the chipping green.

The practice putting green is your friend. It will help you get your speeds dialed-in before the round starts. Don't worry about how many people are on the green, and how many holes there are, or the social niceties as far as putting into another guy's hole (that got awkward quickly). All that you want to do while you are on the practice green is to figure out what it takes to roll a ball ten feet on a level spot. Find a spot on the putting green that looks level, or about level, and pace off three to three and a half paces. Then run that putt back and forth a few times. Do the same with a twenty-foot putt -- nearly seven paces. Again, if there's not a hole to let you do that, don't sweat it. There's no course that has a magic putting green, that has a genie pop out and bless you with immaculate touch if you make five putts in a row. There's no breakthrough that's coming if you aim at a practice cup. And slope is largely slope. If the right side is higher than the left, it's going to break right to left (and the opposite is true, too!) but speed is going to vary a whole lot. If you can spend five to fifteen minutes putting balls back and forth on a green before your round, it will help put you in the mindset of what you are going to need to do out on the course.

Now you have a lot to take in when you are on the green during your round and you need to be fairly quick about it. Slow play is quickly killing the fun of golf and you need to be part of the solution (more on that later). A big element of that is the slowdown around the green.

Do not wait for it to be your turn to putt in order to read the green. The moment you get near the green you should be analyzing what your putt is going to do. Is it uphill or downhill? Can you tell if there's any sort of grain? Overall, does the green slope a certain way? Where are your playing partners' balls? You don't want to step on them when analyzing the scene.

Some people advocate walking past the hole and looking back at your ball, but I'm personally not a fan. The small amount of detail you are going to pick up from doing that is not worth the time spent to walk across the green. Besides, few non-professional golfers can grasp the subtle nuances that looking at a putt from multiple sides can give you.

All that said, if looking at a putt from the other side of the hole is your thing and it works, keep doing it. Whatever works for you -- I'm just trying to pick up the pace by eliminating the superfluous.

Last thing on putting. Always mark your ball, give it a wipe if it's dirty, and when it is time to set it back down on the green, use any indication line on the ball to give your read a definitive line. Every golf ball manufacturer puts some sort of words on the ball (usually a decent sized string of letters in small font, so it resembles a line of some sort). But some companies actually put arrows on the ends of that line of text, to further help your brain see it and use it for alignment purposes. Or, for a dollar you can buy a marker and make your own line. That line will help you immensely because most of us can't make perfectly straight lines out of curved objects, and that's exactly what a ball is. I can't tell you the number of putts I've seen missed over the years that were read properly, and hit properly, but the player's feet were aligned fifteen degrees off. They didn't realize that the ball was pointed the wrong way. Take an extra four seconds, make sure the line or stripe is pointing where you want it to, and then knock that thing in the cup.

Then do it a hundred thousand more times.

Practice With A Purpose

Before I got my first job, I got a junior range pass to Adobe Dam Family Golf Center. It's a range in North Phoenix that has stadium lighting and stays open late. Before I had responsibilities of adulthood, I would go there for hours on end. My mom would drop me off and, five hours later, she'd pick me up. Eventually I got a driver's license and I'd drive myself.

I can't tell you the number of times I drove home, smearing blood on the steering wheel from hitting balls until blisters formed and burst. Actually, I can tell you. It happened twice. I was that stupid, exactly twice. I was nearly that stupid a few dozen more times. I used to bang out range balls like it was my job. And business was booming.

Unfortunately, what I was doing was terrible practice. I'd methodically work my way through my bag, until I'd hit each club perfectly (or at least really well) five times in a row.

Jeff Beck

Why was that a bad idea?

Because that *literally never happens on a golf course*. If you ever hit the same club five times in a row, you've made mistakes on a global level that I can't even begin to fathom. As a part-time novelist, I definitely have an oversized imagination and I'm drawing a blank to come up with a plausible circumstance that sees you hit the same club five shots in a row. There's very few cases where you'd ever hit the same club twice in a row, and decidedly fewer cases where you'd go three times around. It just doesn't make any sense to practice that way.

That didn't stop me from grabbing a jumbo bucket and a Gatorade, followed by another round of jumbo bucket and Gatorade (because it was summer in Phoenix and 110 degrees outside on a cool day. I was stupid, but not *that* stupid). I was unaware that I was doing virtually nothing but working through some puberty-inflicted aggression on some beat-to-hell off-brand range balls.

It sure felt good, though. If that sounds at all familiar, don't worry. Damn near everybody does it. Or at least, they did do it. Then they had a breakthrough (or a breakdown) and figured out a better way. Or they stopped hitting the range altogether.

So instead of just pointing out what I did that was

92

very wrong, and telling you to be better, here's a better method. This is for an actual focused practice session, or the five to fifteen minutes you'll spend warming up on the range before a round.

First, stretch a little. Yeah, when I was twenty-three I didn't need that either, but in my thirties, stretching is nice. I can't imagine what's in store for me in another couple decades -- which makes Roe McBurnett shooting in the 70s while he's in his 80s just that much more impressive. You don't need to make stretching your new hobby. A little bit goes a long way, but keep your first five to ten swings light and easy.

Start with a wedge. Sand, pitch, lob, gap, I really don't care. What you should be looking for is a short shaft, heavy club head, and a three-quarters swing, just to get the blood moving a little bit. If you've worked with a pro and they've given you a drill to work on, give your drill a whirl. Now work through your bag, hitting a few short irons, mid irons, a couple long irons if you've got them, maybe a few hybrids or fairway woods from the ground, then tee a couple up. Next grab your driver, first nice and smooth, then try to kill one or two of them.

That should have you plenty warmed up to go start your round, and if that's the case, have a good round. Go have some fun and I hope you play well.

However, if you aren't playing today, and simply going to practice, and I mean a real *practice* session, then you are just getting started.

First, pull out your yardage book. It can be from anywhere. If you play at a course that has yardage books, phenomenal. It's great to base this practice session on a course you've played before, but it's not mandatory. There's plenty of yardage books for famous courses for sale online and they will work just fine.

If you aren't familiar, a yardage book is an illustrated version of each hole, with specific yardages both to the center of the green from virtually every discernible spot on the hole, as well as from specialized spots to other spots. For example, a yardage book will show the distance from each set of tees to where the fairway ends and the lake begins, as well as how far it is to carry the lake from each tee (and how far across the lake it is in case you decided to play it short), that type of thing. I've seen black and white ones, I've seen leather-bound full colored ones -- it really doesn't matter which one you have. All that matters is that you know how to read it and that you are honest with yourself as you are hitting shots on the range.

94

At this point, you are going to play the course on the range. Pull out the book, and envision that you are on the first tee. It's a 380-yard par four? Great, hit driver. Did you hit it well, and where you wanted? Perfect. The next ball you are going to hit is going to be from 130 yards, since your driver went 250 yards. Or did you miss it a little? Then your second shot needs to be your 140-yard club. If you hit that well, and on target, then congratulations, you hit the green in two. Count it as a par and move on.

If you left your second shot short, hit it long, yanked it left, or faded it right, then you aren't done. Grab a wedge, and pitch or chip it to the middle of the green and provided that you like how that shot went down, move on.

The key to making this work is being honest with yourself. Bad shots are bad shots, they don't reflect you as a person. You can acknowledge that you hit a shot poorly and no one will think less of you.

You don't need to keep score, but you should play all the way through the round. And you should use this opportunity to get your pre-shot routine nailed down. Consistency and brevity are equally important with a pre-shot routine. If you spend four minutes on your pre-shot routine, even if you hit the perfect shot every time, that's not good.

I played in a lot of Junior Golf Association of Arizona tournaments growing up in Phoenix. I never did even remotely well in any of them, but the JGAA was a great way to play a lot of golf at different courses and meet a lot of very uptight kids. It's cool, I can say that. I was one of them.

Parents were able to tag along, if they were to act as the player's caddie. There was one round I played with a kid, whose dad was playing looper and sports psychologist. This guy was like a bad version of Earl Woods (if you aren't familiar, from an early age, Tiger's dad did all sort of things to toughen his son up mentally and to treat the game of golf like going to war), with flawed methods and a substantially-less talented child. And one thing he hammered home (and he hammered that point often and hard) was that his son needed a rock-solid pre-shot routine.

It looked like this. He'd address the ball, but before placing the club down, he'd take a half step back, then take two practice swings. Each one had a several second delay before it started, as the kid debated the big questions in life. Then he'd stand behind the ball, so that the ball was between him and the hole, and he'd take two more practice swings. This time while staring at the pin like he was going to conquer that flagstick's homeland.

Then he'd move back to the first position and take one more practice swing.

Then he'd move back behind the ball again for one last practice swing.

Then he'd hit the ball and, roughly 85 percent of the time, he would hit the ground at least an inch behind the ball, advancing things only sixty or seventy yards. Which was cool, because then we'd get to watch the whole production again after just a short walk down the hole. It was perhaps the most fun I have ever had on a golf course.

Six practice swings from four different locations, on every single swing. The kid shot in the high 90s, so when you count practice swings and actual swings, he was flirting with a 650 swings or so for 18 holes.

That kid's back is still sore.

I'm all for a pre-shot routine. I'm all for consistency. I'm also all for a sub-four hour round.

If you are a practice-swing kind of golfer, that's great. I am. If you aren't, also great. I've spent time doing that as well. Whatever you are, just embrace it. And if you are into the practice swing, just one will suffice. If something happened during your practice swing, like your playing partner suffered a heart attack or an adjacent car backfired, then take another one. But all things being equal, one practice swing is plenty.

Are we good? Ready to stop abusing the practice swing? Awesome, let's get back to the range.

There's two things that most golfers don't realize they should be doing on the range, regardless of their intention. The first is ball placement, the second is stall choice.

Ball placement deals with where you place each ball on the range. I know, it sounds crazy, but there's a right way, and a wrong way, and it's all because of your divot.

You should take a divot (of varying depth and size) with most well-struck iron shots, and perhaps even hybrid or fairway wood shots too. But the divot happens after you impact the ball -- the golf swing sees the club descend through the ball and into the ground.

Because of that, you can effectively reuse the same spot over and over again. Wherever you start hitting balls, try to pick a location that has decent grass going directly back from it, for at least a foot or two. Then hit your first shot, which should create a full-sized divot. That's the start of your line. Your second ball should be placed right at the back side of your previous divot, so that your second swing will only take a small piece of grass, before it gets to the divot your first swing made.

It takes a little while to get used to, but it is a much more efficient way to go instead of just randomly placing each ball somewhere in your stall. If there isn't any order, you'll end up taking full-sized divots all over the place. If you take the stripe all the way back to the end of your stall, start a new one right next to where you started the first one. I've seen the result of a player, with proper range usage, hit in one stall for hours and a quarter of his stall was completely picked clean of grass and the rest was untouched. Doing so can help you (for alignment purposes) as much as it helps everyone else who is going to use the stall after you. And the staff will thank you as well.

The other thing to keep in mind is where to pick your stall on the range. Granted, if there's only one spot open, that's where you are headed. But if you have a choice, don't just settle for what's available or the closest walk (even if it means hanging out for a couple minutes while people wrap up their practice or warmup session). The best stall for you is all based on your ball flight.

If you hit the ball right-to-left (or even center-to-left), that's called a draw when it is subtle and in control, but when it goes out control, that's called a hook. If you hit the ball left-to-right, that's a fade, but when it goes extremely left-to-right, it is termed a slice. If you are left-handed, reverse all of that.

Most people who fight a slice tend to take a spot all the way on the left end of the range, so when they slice it they go across the range. Sadly, they couldn't be further from the spot they should be in. Bear with me.

A slicer, who is a person who hits a slice (much like a hooker is someone who hits a hook according to at least forty different golf jokes that are equally hilarious), should set up on the furthest right stall they can get and aim across the range to the left. The thought process is, that they should plan on hitting a fade most of the time and when it gets unruly, (and their right-to-left action takes the fade to the next level and slices more than they would like) everything is still fine because they are aiming at the right place.

I know, you're screaming at me right now, "But Jeff, if I stayed on the left side of things and just aimed down the left edge, it'd do the same thing!", except that's not true.

SUCK LESS AT GOLF

A fade, or slice, typically happens because of an outside-in swing path. Much like a sand shot, or a flop shot, your club path is not a straight back and through. That imparts side-spin on the ball. If the club head is square and you are outside-in, you'll see a fade, but if the club head is open and you are outside-in, that's when the slice shows up. The reason you don't want to be on the left edge is because of what happens when you have a closed club face and are outside-in.

That's what we like to call a pull (we like to call it that because that's what it's called). It's a straight shot that goes straight down the third base foul line, or even further to the left. And if you are a regular slicer, you likely hit them with some regularity. Which means on the range, you are losing balls for the range (all depending on where your range is located). By sticking to stalls on the right side of the range and hitting across the range, a pull should still land in the grass, keeping the facility from losing balls every time you show up (and keeping you out of windshield breaking litigation).

Everything I've said comes into play for folks with an inside-out swing, square face is a draw, closed face is hook, open face is a push. Which means you should set up on the left side of the range, and aim toward the right-hand side.

Make sure that you have a target and always be aware of your alignment.

Far too many golfers, myself included (in my younger years), just bang out balls on the range. Grooving their swing, or releasing aggression, or whatever, but they aren't putting much, if any, thought into each swing. That's less than ideal.

You should pick a spot on the range and hit toward it. That's why ranges have target greens with flags -- nobody actually gets anything for hitting a great shot, but it helps you focus on what you should be hitting at. Don't sweat it if your target is the wrong depth, i.e. the flag is at 150 yards and you are hitting your 100-yard club, or your 180-yard club. As long as your 100-yard shot comes down in line with the 150-yard pin, or the 180-yard shot flies over the 150-yard pin, you did what you set out to do. The reason you don't want to just bang balls out without a target is you would never do that on the golf course. Everything you do on the range is in service of what you will do on the course -- except maybe that cool guy bouncing a ball on the wedge trick, which I used to do walking up and down the hallway in my dorm, to prove just how cool I was (in case you were wondering how insufferable I was to be around in my early twenties) -- so you need to find a target for every shot.

The other half of that nugget is to ensure that you are properly lined up to your target. If you are out on the range alone, then you don't really have any options. Staring down at your feet, trying to ascertain where they are pointing, can be misleading. Especially if you have recently changed a part of your swing -- and certainly if you've changed your stance in some way.

One way to combat this is with baby powder. I wouldn't recommend doing this if you are only warming up for a round, but if you have a solid practice session coming, pick out your main target for the day, and lay a club down on the ground pointing directly to it. Then take the baby powder and draw a line down the shaft, so you have a perfectly straight line, pointing directly at your target. From then on out, you just need to make sure that your toes are equidistant to the line from each other (or close enough) and you'll know that you are on target.

Or you could make a friend.

The Buddy System

Golf is a solitary sport. Every now and then a team event happens, like the Ryder Cup, where the best golfers in the world have to play together in a forced cooperative environment. Some of the guys seem to love it and others look like they are being tortured in front of a gallery.

I get it. This is one of those sports where only you can affect you and relying on someone else flies in the face of everything you've ever learned.

That doesn't mean you shouldn't have golfing buddies. More than one is great, but one is plenty. A golfing buddy is more than someone you sporadically play with -- a golfing buddy knows your game and ideally is just a little bit better than you are. Maybe you guys hit the range together, or ask each other for advice. I know what you're thinking. It sounds like pre-teen girls where you braid each other's hair and talk about what you want to do after college, but it's not.

My golfing buddy is named Todd. We were fraternity

brothers in college and we both got the same job in Hawaii caddying at the same time. Todd loves golf more than other person I know, and in the nearly twenty years I've known him, he's never once turned down an offer to go hit range balls or play a quick nine.

Things have changed quite a bit since college. He's now a hell of a golfer, who could give me somewhere between five and seven stokes a side and still beat me, but back in the college years he was only slightly better than me. We likely had a 60/40 split of his wins to mine. Very little of that was based on me. My game has always been very pedestrian. Lots of pars, very consistent, and on a good day, boring. He was all about birdies and bogeys. On the days when he had a few of the former and a lot of the latter, I'd win handily. When the reverse would happen, I wouldn't have a chance. Our matches rarely ended close.

The reason I'd encourage each of you to find your own Todd (besides not having to be the guy who shows up to play as a single, and intrudes on a pre-made threesome) is that he knew my swing and my game, better than anyone that wasn't me. Whenever my game has been struggling in some manner, he can usually diagnose it pretty quickly. It would usually be something simple that I was just *missing* and another set of eyes could catch it. Everyone's golf swing is different, so asking an outside source for a quick problem assessment is worthless. If they don't know what things going well looks like, how can they have any idea what minor glitch is throwing everything off?

I went through a short phase where I developed the shanks on chip shots, and in turn, only pitched the ball. Regardless of the situation, Todd called me out on it. Having someone act as a de facto golf mentor is helpful, no matter who you are.

Part of that, however, means giving back as well. It means paying attention to the other person's swing and pointing out after the round (either because you don't want to mess with their game while on the course, or you don't want to help fix them, when you have a four stroke lead with two holes to go -- we may never know your true motivations) that they were lifting their left heel at the top of their swing, and what's up with that? Another one of the guys I worked with when I was outside service, and eventually also became a fraternity brother, was named Big Matt. Big Matt had a unique philosophy that he espoused, frequently.

The world is a wheel. There are a million ways that play

into the game of golf, but the abridged version is, that you need to be aware of your surroundings. Make sure that for every nice thing someone does for you, that you are doing something for someone else too.

Your golf buddy doesn't exist to make sure that your game is up to snuff. He isn't there to keep you in ball marks and tees. He's also not the pace bunny to set the standard. He's your friend, first and foremost, and if he's helping you out -- make sure you're passing it on. Maybe you pass it back to him or maybe the good deeds go to someone else. Golf is a selfish and singular game, but that doesn't mean it needs to turn you into a selfish and singular person.

Jeff Beck

Course Management

I know. The moment we've all been waiting for.

Course management is the single biggest change you can make to your game and, using good course management can decrease your score. Good course management can lead to a round where you hit the ball poorly, yet scored well. Bad course management is what happens when you hit the ball well and scored terribly.

I've done both, plenty of times. It feels far better to score well on bad shots. It feels like you got one over on the universe. By all rights, you should have scored a 96, yet somehow, you're drinking a beer with an 81 on your card. Sure, it would have been nicer if you'd hit every drive pure, and stuffed every approach shot to four feet, but that ain't you most days. And it certainly wasn't you today.

You conned the golf course. And this wasn't just that thing where you had a weird tweener sixty-yard approach shot that took one hop and jumped into the cup. This

108

took all day. This was The Long Con.

Course management is the generic term for playing smart golf. Roe McBurnett's game was 100 percent golf course management, but when I'd talk to him about it, he'd shake his head. That was just his way of playing. And maybe it came naturally to him, after playing for decades, or maybe he learned it along the way. Either way, he never lost sight of the goal. Score well.

My high school job selling golf clubs was right across the street from the Peoria Sports Complex, the Spring Training home of the Seattle Mariners and San Diego Padres. We had a few players come by to check out or buy new clubs from time to time. One guy, a pitcher we'll call Arnold, who'd had Tommy John surgery (a surgery that has a lengthy recovery time that involves taking a ligament from a pitcher's non-throwing arm and putting it into their throwing arm following a blow out of the original ligament) and was looking at a huge amount of rehab. He moved to Phoenix early and got a job with us, long before Spring Training started. He was bored, loved golf and golf club discounts (along with a small hookup we had with a nearby course), which meant he didn't mind working a few shifts a week, in between physical therapy sessions.

Jeff Beck

I've never seen someone make the wind whistle just by casually moving their hand, but this guy could. I watched him throw a golf ball 92 miles per hour, half-heartedly and without much of a windup (we had a hitting simulator that measured ball speed in the shop -- I wasn't holding a radar gun or anything). Turns out, Major League Baseball pitchers can throw a sphere pretty fast. Arnold could also hit the ball a country mile off the tee, but he had some slight accuracy issues. By slight, I mean that the ball could go literally in any direction.

The flip side of that, is that he could hit the ball far. Stupidly far. Three-hundred and fifty yards or more far. Dude could hit it. And when he hit it straight, or straight-ish, it was a sight to see. And his wedge game was rock solid. Maybe not PGA Tour level of solid, but much better than most other amateurs.

Problem was, his drives could go all over the place (when you hit it that far, a little off target line becomes a *lot* off target), but more importantly, his wedges went way too far. He wasn't blading sand wedges 140 yards, he was hitting them purely and they'd go that far. I watched that same sand wedge land on the back of a massive green and back all the way off of it. Arnold put enough zip on a ball to back it up 25 yards.

SUCK LESS AT GOLF

Do you see the flaw in his game yet?

There's an awful lot of golf played from 135 yards and in. Some would argue (and I would say that they are correct) that the most important golf is played in that zone. And he didn't have anything that would go that length. He hit the ball so hard that he was playing a different game than the rest of us. Sure, he could have dialed back his swing intensity, and he probably would have increased his accuracy by magnitudes, but where is the fun in that?

No clue what ended up happening to him. After he finished his rehab, I'd catch a highlight with him on *SportsCenter* and think about the number of times he'd outdriven me by 80 yards, on a particular hole, only to lose by a stroke or three.

Arnold needed course management. He needed someone to pick apart his game, identify his strengths and weaknesses, and then game plan how to leverage his strengths to cover his weaknesses.

You've already got a head start there. A few chapters ago, I told you to identify your money club, and then work on how to integrate it into your game more often. We've already talked about the short game, and playing the highest probability of success shot, instead of the once-in-a-lifetime shot. So much of course management is being honest with yourself and staying within your lane. If you can't hit the ball 300 yards, stop trying to do so. Not only is it not going to happen, you're going to wear yourself out trying. And if, by some stroke of luck, it does, you won't know what to do once you get there. Unless you are one of the top 200 golfers in the world, you cannot bend the course to your will. You cannot overpower it. The course is Goliath and you are David. You have to outsmart it. Use your strengths to make the course work for you -- or start playing a course that works to your advantage.

Are you super accurate, but not very long? Play tight courses that require precision, either with a million trees or lots of water. Put your playing partners on edge, while you simply dink and dunk your way through the round, as they sail their ball into ponds and lakes.

Is your sand game among the top ten in the world? Make that your advantage and encourage your group to play courses with nasty bunkers. A little course knowledge can be a wonderful thing. There's a course in Northwest Phoenix, (nearly all the way out of town) called Blackstone. It's a desert course, but it's a Jim Engh design. Like most of Engh's designs, he put a ton of hills around the greens. That may sound less than ideal, but in reality, it means that wayward approach shots have a decent chance to get a lucky kick and end up on the green. If you *really* miss it, then yes, you are going to land on the opposite side of the hill and it will kick you even further from the green. But if you miss a little? You may find yourself putting all day.

But back to your game and course management. You need to take a hard look at your sticks. How well do you hit your long irons? If you don't have confidence that you will hit a club well, it has no place in your bag. If you don't have confidence that you will hit any club well, you need to spend more time practicing until you have at least a little confidence. I spent years lugging a three-iron around, because it came with my set of irons. But every time I'd try to do something with it, it would end somewhere between catastrophic and awful. I should have left that thing in the garage years earlier, but I didn't because the optimist in me said that the next time I hit it, all my woes would go away and my three-iron and I would be best friends.

I was an idiot. Don't emulate me.

Remove everything that is standing in your way. If that means you only show up with ten to twelve clubs in your bag, so be it. The maximum allowed is fourteen and there is no minimum.

Don't be afraid to try something different. Like I said earlier, going seven-iron/seven-iron may be the better play than driver/half-wedge, but you'll never know until you try it. If what you are doing is not working, try something else. Even if it doesn't work, you are still making progress. You can cross two things off the list -- what you normally do and your first option. Next time, you'll try something else.

I would not recommend switching sides and trying to play left-handed, if you are a righty. Sure, Phil Mickelson did, but he started off playing as a little boy, watching himself in the mirror and trying to emulate his dad's swing. I can't imagine that, years into playing golf, anyone would be able to make a switch very easily.

Identify your strongest club or at the very least, your strongest attribute. If you can hit tee shots well, or longer than everyone else in your group, see if you can convince your group to step back one or two tee boxes. If the course is crowded you shouldn't really do this -- people playing the wrong tee greatly contributes to the slow rounds of today. While everyone else is struggling to keep up with you, they will make mistakes. Part of playing better golf is when everyone else is playing worse, you have effectively gotten better. If you tune into the US Open, you'll frequently see the winner shoot right around even par. It's not to say that the field has fallen apart, simply that the tournament organizers took a tough course, then did everything they could to make it harder.

If approach shots are your bread and butter, work on them until they give you an almost unfair advantage. You don't need to improve every aspect of your game if any one aspect is amazing -- except tee shots. If you could hit the ball 300 plus yards every time, and perfectly straight, your scores wouldn't really change by much. But if you hit every green, they would. Or if you knew you could get up and down almost every time -- your scores would come down. We know that the best putters in the world still miss about half the putts they take from ten feet, but they also make almost everything from five feet. Suddenly the hole is effectively five feet big -- now just make it into that range and you are done.

You can get creative with your shots; not everything has to be a standard, full swing. Have you ever hit a punch shot? That is one of those shots that stays low (normally to keep it below the wind) though you can hit a punch to avoid an obstacle as well. It's not hard to pull off. You put the ball back in your stance, shorten your back swing a bit, then don't finish your follow through.

I spent a month hitting nothing but punch shots whenever I needed to hit an iron. It started because my iron game was struggling at the time and I found myself in the woods bordering a hole. I punched it out (I needed to keep it low, so my ball didn't clip one the branches on its way back to the fairway) and I hit the ball perfectly. The contact was crisp, the ball went exactly where I wanted it to, and it felt great. A punch shot will normally take some distance off a normal swing, but if you club up one or two sticks you can get away with it. And, that type of shot usually puts a large amount of spin on the ball. I've never backed up a five-iron, but a well-struck, punched five-iron can snap to a stop faster than any full-swing seven-iron I've ever hit.

Eventually, my iron game came back. I stopped playing like I lived in Texas (you'll find tons of wind in Texas so many golfers from the area favor the punch) and things went back to normal.

Remember Big Matt? Mr. "The World is a Wheel"? There's something else very notable about Big Matt (besides the fact that he introduced me to the Bee-On-A-String trick -- I'm serious. He would catch a bee in a cup, put the cup in the ice maker to let the cold knock the bee unconscious, then tie a string around its mid-section. It's amazing to watch) and that is his way of golf. He's embraced his natural swing, which was a huge slice.

Actually, that's not accurate. It's not a huge slice. It's the biggest slice. Just a monster of a slice, and it wasn't an occasional or sporadic thing. If he hit a golf ball, it sliced. He sliced woods and irons, but he also sliced wedges. He sliced sand wedges. I never asked him about fixing it, but he didn't fight it. He leaned into it. Even though he routinely cost himself a solid forty to sixty yards off of every tee, he figured out how to play his game, and routinely shoots in the high-seventies to low-eighties.

Every now and then he'd find a way to leverage it to an advantage (every dogleg right hole, where he could boomerang his ball around the corner and get a fifty-yard advantage over everybody), but for the most part, it was just his burden to bear. He didn't bitch about it -- much -- and when he did it was largely a joke. Yeah, he could have changed his swing to reduce or perhaps get rid of his slice altogether, but that's a lot of time spent at the range. While the slice hurt his distance, it didn't hurt his game overall. That's part of his game's charm -- you've never seen a four-iron land so softly on the green as a sliced Big

Matt four-iron.

He could have buried his head in the sand and convinced himself that the next shot wasn't going to slice, but he would find himself playing out of the woods, other peoples' backyards, or the next fairway over but instead, he always knows what is coming and makes it work.

And that's what you need to do. You have to be objectively honest about your ability as a golfer if you want to play better golf. You don't have to tell anyone else what your weaknesses are, but you have to remove any rose-colored glasses that you might be wearing if you really want to improve. That's not easy. We don't like hearing bad things about ourselves and most of us are our own worst critic about many things. Having a weak short game isn't a character flaw -- it's likely a reflection that you don't put much time into your short game. Unless you do spend a large amount of time around the chipping green and still have no touch whatsoever -- that *is* actually a character flaw and I hate to say it, but you are a bad person.

Stop. You aren't. You just need help, or you need to take some pressure off yourself.

RELAX

You have to stop caring so damn much about golf.

Ironic, isn't it? But it's true. So much of what makes golf hard is the pressure we put on ourselves to make the perfect shot.

Before I wrote my first book, I read everything I could find about writing books. The best advice I picked up (besides "write every single day"), was "the perfect book is the enemy of the good book." I completely understand that. You can spend a lifetime tinkering on one book and, perhaps long before you ultimately publish it, you actually had it at it's best point -- but it wasn't perfect so you kept tinkering. Ultimately, you ended up with a lesser story because you couldn't get out of your own way.

Golf is like that. You can hit it 260 yards to the right side of the fairway of a dogleg right and be happy, or you can it 260 yards to the right of the fairway of a dogleg right and be angry. Sure, you wish it had gone further, maybe 280 or more, or perhaps you wanted to be on the left side of the fairway so you had a better angle at the green. Well, I hate to break it to you, but it didn't go like that. It went 260 and it's on the right side. And now you don't have a direct shot at the green.

If you throw an internal hissy fit over what transpired, it won't help.

If you throw an external hissy fit, it's going to end even worse. Shit happens. You aren't a child. No one needs a temper tantrum of any kind -- not those throwing it and certainly not those watching it. Move on.

You don't have a shot at the green, so you have a few options to choose from. Here's where you get to exercise your course management skills.

A. Hit a wedge at whatever angle will leave a wedge or so in -- be sure not to go too far and leave yourself a half club in.

B. Throw caution to the wind and take the club that will get you home, distance-wise. Aim just to the left of the tree line, hoping to hit some sort of monster fade/power slice that will bring the ball back to the green.

C. Suck your thumb and cry in the corner.

A or B are your best bets. While I'd say A is the safer play if you can hit a fade with some consistency, trying to force a slice and make B happen isn't an awful option.

See how easy that was?

You have no idea how many golfers I've spoken with who have anxiety over playing golf with other people. Especially teeing off on the first tee, when there are other groups around. It's like tee shots are the new public speaking. Some people tolerate it, while many others are white knuckled the whole time. And much like public speaking in school, most people are too nervous themselves to care about whatever it is that you did. Hit your shot, do your thing, and RELAX.

There are no real consequences on a golf course. The closest thing to a consequence only occurs if you are playing a course with homes on it, and you break a window. Legally speaking, you just bought a nice new window for someone else's home. But putting a ball into a lake costs you a stroke and a ball, and that's not so bad. Putting the ball into the sand doesn't mean that someone is going to key your car or punch you in the mouth. Three-putting from eight feet doesn't mean that you are getting divorced (unless your spouse is a monster, in which case I say good riddance).

Those things are real consequences and golf doesn't have consequences. You can create them artificially, by betting $1,000, when you only have $37 to your name. You better win. But that was a choice that you made. You did that. Golf didn't do that to you.

The reason I'm making this point is, the more you stress about golf, the worse you are going to play. Most of us (well, pretty much all of us) aren't professional athletes. We don't thrive under pressure. Except, most professional athletes don't really thrive under pressure -- they've just gotten better at focusing on what matters.

There's not a player on the PGA Tour that stands over a putt on the 72nd hole of a tournament, thinking "If I make this putt, I win. I win the millions of dollars in prize money, not to mention the added endorsement potential, fan adoration, and everything else. This putt is very important."

No. They are standing over the putt thinking, "On Thursday, the cup was over there, and when my ball came through here, it didn't break at all. On Friday, I was paired with Jenson and his putt went right from here, and there was a fair amount of break, but that cup was in the wrong direction from where I'm going. Yesterday I chipped in, but during the practice rounds, my caddie and I spent forty minutes on this green, and I know that this putt is going to be just a bit uphill, and somewhere between right edge and a half-ball outside right edge."

The Tour pro's caddie isn't weighing in on what color Ferrari the pro should buy to commemorate his victory. If he says anything, it'll be something like "You have to go outside of the hole, I think. Unless you want to play it just a bit firmer, then aim right at the edge."

They are thinking and talking about everything but the big picture. If you look at the big picture, it can overwhelm you. It's the same reason that extreme athletes are able to do anything. There's a mountain bike trail up in Sedona, Arizona called White Line and, if you aren't familiar with it, look it up. It's a short trail that goes out on the side of a cliff, then you ride down an extremely steep section about twenty feet and ride back to safety on a second small trail. I've never ridden it (and I never will) but I know a few guys who have. They call it "The Sidewalk to Heaven," because it's about the width of a sidewalk and, if you mess it up, you will probably die. Why does anyone do it? Well, I don't know the answer to that, but I know exactly *how* they do it. They convince themselves that they've ridden on a sidewalk a million times and have never had an issue, so this time, they will not have an issue. Just because there's a consequence, it doesn't change the action required. Making a five-foot putt with nothing on the line, or everything on the line, requires the exact same motion.

Feel free to experiment with things. You cannot find new ways to do things if you don't take chances. And you may find that your attempt at trying something new is now your regular way of doing things. You may find that your game resembles my golf buddy Todd's game, where you trade bogeys and birdies frequently, and hope for a good exchange rate. Or you may find that playing the conservative game, striving for par and limiting your exposure, is your most effective way to get around the course.

If you want to aim for the pin, then aim for the pin, even if it is tucked behind a bunker. So what if it lands in the sand. You'll get out. If you don't, you didn't encounter a negative consequence so much as you learned something.

You need to park your heels in the practice bunker and spend an hour or two chopping at golf balls.

On the Full Swing

I've said all along that I wasn't going to give swing advice in this book. I cannot properly tell you where your elbow should be at the top of your swing, because I have no idea what your swing looks like, or how well it works for you. Maybe dropping your elbow will ruin your swing completely, so we're not going to go there. What I will tell you is that you need to stop trying to hit the ball straight. Much like Big Matty, you need to play your game, and be it a slight fade or a slight draw, embrace it. It will help you.

Remember the thing about the shape of your swing being outside-in, resulting in a fade, or inside-out, resulting in a draw? Those aren't swing flaws. Those are swing features. Hear me out.

It is far easier to replicate a deliberate swing. By deliberate, I mean the thought, "I want to hit a little fade here," so you match your swing just ever so slightly outside-in. If you end up a little further outside-in than you anticipated, it just means that the ball is going to move a little more than you wanted. It's still going to go the way you intended. Or your swing could go the other way and it isn't as outside-in as you had planned on, and as a result the ball barely moves in the air. That's fine. The premise is, you've aimed a little left of where you want the ball to be and if the ball moves a little more or less than what you were going for, it isn't going to hurt you much. If at all.

There's a highly unlikely chance that you are going to double-cross yourself (which is when you play for a fade and then you hit a draw). Your swing would have to be completely out of control for that to happen. But if you are playing for a straight shot and your swing ends up just a bit inside or a bit outside, your shot pattern will be all over the place. Sometimes you are well left or right, and you can't count on what your next shot will do.

This is the full swing equivalent of the "how the hell do I know how the hell hard I'm going to hit a putt?" conundrum.

There isn't a member of any Tour, be it PGA, LPGA, or Senior PGA that hits a straight shot as a default swing. They all hit a fade or a draw on purpose.

If you are actively shaping your swing to produce one

or the other (and a draw by definition will normally go farther) you should try to hit a draw, right?

You might not want to do that.

It is true that a draw will normally go a little further than a fade. A fade is the result of the club face being open (or the equivalent swing pattern), which means that the club is adding loft and the shot is going higher. A draw (being the opposite) is the clubface closing down, de-lofting the club, and going lower.

But we aren't talking about massive differences here. If your normal drive goes 250 when it's straight, a faded drive will go 245-250 and a draw will go 250-255. Not life changing numbers.

However, a draw will land hotter, which means that it is harder to stop. Great from the tee, but less than ideal when hitting your approach shots. Meanwhile, a faded five-iron will come to rest far more quickly than a five-iron with a draw on it. That could be worth sacrificing a little bit of distance.

Not that it is always so easy to just decide what you are going to do. For years, I had what could only be described (generously) as a flawed swing. There were too many things wrong with it to focus on just six or seven different aspects. It was messed up. But I had good touch and good tempo and I could usually make it work, if I didn't get ahead of myself. With some professional help, I reworked my swing, simplified it in a number of ways, and it changed my game, mostly for the better.

I went from a fade to a draw. I was the envy of the neighborhood -- except it messed my game up. It took years to get back to shooting the same numbers I was before because everything was wrong or, at least, everything felt backward. My strategies for playing certain holes no longer worked. Lakes or trees that were never a consideration now factored into my style of play.

It wasn't quite as jarring as if I'd switched over to playing left-handed, but it sure felt like it. Eventually I got through my head how I should approach certain holes, and I got my game sorted out. But the hard part came when the wheels came off the wagon.

When I played the fade, things rarely went very wrong. Once in a blue moon, I'd get outside of my swing and hit a full-fledged slice. I didn't fear the banana ball for the same reason I'm not afraid to fly on airplanes -- the numbers just don't support it. One slice every couple of months wasn't anything to think about.

But when I switched to a draw, the worst case scenario version, the hook, wasn't nearly as elusive. All I needed to do was get a little quick with any aspect of my swing -- my backswing, the almost imperceivable delay at the top, accelerating into the front swing -- my shoulders and hips would get their signals crossed and my swing path would come inside-out too far by a few degrees. As a result, I'd hit a snap hook that would out relatively straight but, forty yards into the shot it would make a dramatic left-handed turn.

In my previous life, I had to fight to hit a slice out to the far right, and suddenly I was up to my ankles in hooks, seeing the left side of courses I'd spent years ignoring. Maybe not the best move I've ever made. The extra length off the tee was nice (except when a ball ran through the fairway, which was suddenly an option), but watching my eight-iron run off of the back of any green, (at least any eight-iron that wasn't well struck -- I could still stop it if I clipped it right) was frustrating.

So this isn't as much about picking one side and sticking to it so much as acknowledging the characteristics of your swing and using them to your advantage. Find your inner Big Matty and lean into whatever swing you have.

On the Course

Golf is dying. It has had its ups and downs over the last few decades, but it has been steadily dwindling for the past ten years. You can blame over-saturation of too many golf courses, or you could blame the economy reducing golfers' disposable incomes, but as golf courses have shut down and the economy has improved, those excuses went out the window.

The real culprit is time. It takes too long to play a round of golf. We live in a world where we have all gotten used to instant gratification. You can order a product from your phone and have it delivered to your home in the next two hours. If a customer service email doesn't get answered the same day, many of us run to social media to air our grievances and cry foul.

In addition, there are more options today to occupy your time than ever before, which makes spending a full four hours of your free time on the course a tough sell. Sure, the cost of green fees ticking up isn't helping matters, but money is relative. Some folks won't think twice about dropping $150 for eighteen holes, while others would never spend that on one round in their life. But time is the great equalizer. We all get twenty-four hours in the day and spending four of those hours playing a round of golf requires committment.

Especially because it's not four hours any more. In order to play a round of golf, more often than not, you are actually closer to five hours. And that's just time on the course. Never mind the time warming up at the range. Or on the practice green. Or driving to the course. Or grabbing a drink and a bite after the round, or the drive home. Depending on your travel, a round of golf has turned into a six-to-eight-hour experience that you paid a non-insignificant amount of money for.

If you are single, maybe that's how you wanted to spend your Saturday. If you are married, or have a significant other, having a weekly round of golf requires a lot of compromise. Most people in a relationship like actually spending time with their significant others.

Then add kids into the mix. The majority of the disposable time that you used to have just evaporated. Sneaking away for six hours in order to play a round of golf with your friends just became a whole lot harder.

Special occasion levels of harder.

And there's no reason for the game to take so long. The game of golf hasn't changed in a way that should make a round take longer. In fact, with the addition of better clubs and balls, people should be playing better and faster. GPS locators on carts mean that the rounds should be even faster. And yet they aren't.

That's your fault. Not solely yours, but you are a part of the problem. Every single one of us who steps foot on the course has a hand in the pace. All it takes is one bad group to slow things down. Hell, the entire group doesn't need to be slow, just one slow golfer can affect an entire course. If that slow golfer had an early tee time, he or she has messed up an entire day. Much like a traffic accident on the highway ten minutes before rush hour starts, the trickle-down effect will be felt for hours, and there's no way to get that delay back. Once the time is spent, you can't reclaim it. You need to do everything in your power to ensure that your group isn't the one messing it up for everyone else.

Before you launch into an angry email telling me that it's never your fault, stop. I know. I know that most people really aren't at fault. I worked in golf long enough to know that most golfers aren't the culprit. But I'm painting everyone with broad-enough strokes knowing that the guilty parties will get some on them too. Unfortunately, most of them are going to think they are absolved of blame too.

Slow golf isn't solely the fault of slow golfers. Ultimately, it starts with the course itself. There are two things courses can do to stack the deck in their favor. One of them is longer intervals between tee times, and the other is an effective ranger.

The longer you go between groups, the less overall people will be on a golf course. That's simple logic. At Forest Highlands, our gaps were 10 minutes long and that worked pretty well. At Nanea, they were 15 minutes. At Troon North, they alternated between 7 minutes and 8 minutes, and that little change down from 10 minutes made all the difference in the world. That's starting out on a sour note. Set yourself up to win, or set yourself up to lose -- and a short interval is setting yourself up to lose.

A good ranger can save the day. Ultimately, a good ranger needs to employ what my dad has always referred to as "the steel hand inside the velvet glove." They need to threaten the guilty party, (and have the course's endorsement to make that threat) but they need to do it in a way that doesn't make the slow player angry, and instead, inspires them to speed up. A good ranger excels at reading people. They need the ability to figure out, on the fly, the best way to approach a situation.

Good rangers are rare.

The issue is, most golf courses do not allow their rangers to make any threats whatsoever. Now, when I say "threat" I do not mean anyone is getting stabbed and no one is going to have any of their clubs broken. It's more of forcing a group to either skip one or two holes to get back in position or adopting a new lifestyle where they let every group behind them play through.

The second way is rarely effective though, because if you have seven groups lined up one after another, there's no place for the slow group to resume play. That's why they need to drastically speed up or skip ahead. That that kind of threat is usually only levied after they have been warned numerous times that they need to speed up.

There is something else golf courses can do to help slow play -- but it really only works with a regular membership. You have to identify who the slow players are and restrict their tee time making ability. When I was in the shop, it didn't take long to learn who the single handful of members were that couldn't finish a round in under five hours if you had pointed a gun at them the entire time. Even more frustrating, if you ever spoke to them on the course about their pace, they would get belligerent, nearly to the point of threatening violence. There was only one answer: when one of those members called and asked for an 8:30 tee time, the earliest one we had available wasn't until 11:10. Knowing that, at that time of the year, we were really only busy until 10:30 or 11:00. He could slow play all he liked and only screw up his own day.

That was a functional solution, until we adopted an online tee system, where members could log in and make their own tee times with unlimited access to the tee sheet. We may or may not have artificially filled a number of spots with members who never played (or even had signed up for the program) when we knew that Captain Slowplay was likely to throw his name on the sheet.

I'm not proud of it, but it had to be done for the greater good. Better to have one upset golfer than a few dozen -- especially when that one is the root of the problem.

The best thing you can do to help prevent slow play is incredibly straightforward. Play faster.

It's just that simple.

Tangent time. In Hawaii, the golf shop would send out five-somes, provided it was one of the 361 days of the year that the course wasn't busy. Five-somes are absolutely unheard of in the golf world. At Nanea, it wasn't a big deal -- you just needed to take two caddies with your group to help move things along. They would even consider letting a six-some tee off as well, and so much of that was based on it being the caddies' responsibility to get a group around. Every member knew that if a caddie said "we're holding everything up, we *need* to speed up," it couldn't be shrugged off and it certainly wasn't to be met with resistance. If the caddie said "we are going to stop and let a group play through," that is exactly what was going to happen.

It was awesome. Talk about setting yourself up to win. Slow rounds simply do not exist there.

Every Monday, the course was closed for maintenance. The employees were able to play in the afternoon, when the overhaul maintenance of the day was complete. So we would tee off essentially every single Monday afternoon, oftentimes as a five-some. Occasionally as a six-some (not exactly sure why we didn't play as two threesomes, but I think there was a certain type of betting game going on that relied on everyone being in the same group). I even remember playing once as a part of a nine-some. It was chaotic and awesome, and lasted every bit of four hours and ten minutes. Sure, we were all pretty good golfers to great golfers, but that was still off-the-charts amazing. The reason we were able to get it done so quickly is that every player knew the numerous written and unwritten rules you need to follow in order to play fast golf.

First -- you're there to play golf. If your cell phone is with you, it's silenced or off. If you want to spend the afternoon texting your girlfriend, stay off the course. We'll make fun of you plenty, but it's probably better that everyone makes fun of you behind your back, as opposed to you ruining a whole course's afternoon.

Second -- pay attention to what you, and everyone else, is doing. Some people have the memory of a goldfish. They hit their drive into the right rough, right around the third set of trees, and by the time they have sat down in the cart, they don't remember where their ball is. That's why it's good to keep an eye on your ball, and everyone else's too.

Three -- don't wait until it is your turn to be ready. That means on the tee box, you need to have your club ready. If the tee box is a bit of a walk from your cart and you are on a par-3, bring multiple clubs with you. There is no rule that stipulates you can only take one club out of your bag at a time. If you think it's going to be a six-iron? Bring your five and seven as well. That way, if you have a last second change of heart or the wind kicks up or dies down, it doesn't cost the group a minute or two while you are working through a mountain of self-doubt over how much wind is swirling above you (when in doubt take more club and swing easy). That doesn't sound like much, but with four people in a group, a few last-minute club changes per person can add twenty minutes to a round of golf. You can bring extra clubs with you to your second shot, and you should if you are playing a cart-path-only course or your cart driving buddy has dropped you off and driven on to his ball, making your clubs less than easily accessible. Walking back and forth to your cart is a great way to slow things down and screw up everyone's afternoon.

Four -- read your putt early and often. I'm all for adhering to etiquette and adhering to honors (that is whoever is the furthest out, hit first). I'm not a monster. But it doesn't mean that you should stand there and gaze up, trying to figure out which cloud looks like which animal. You should be reading your putt and trying to figure out what this next shot is going to be. That way, when it is your turn, you can place your ball on the green, pick up your ball mark, take a practice swipe, then run it in.

Five -- play the proper tees. Too many slow groups are only slow because they are putting themselves in the wrong spot at the start of every hole. Or the talent level in the group is mixed and they think it will take longer to have the one or two new golfers tee off from the white tees and just have everyone tee it from the blues or blacks. Play the proper tees. It's not hard to figure out which ones are right for you. If you step up to a par-four and you can't get it around the green with your second shot, you are playing the wrong tees. And I don't mean going driver/five-wood. You should mostly have mid-irons into greens on par-fours.

Six -- walk every now and then. By walking a course, either alone or with a caddie, it becomes very evident that you must always be moving forward in order to keep up. If someone is not in the process of hitting a ball, you should be walking toward your ball or the green. Riding in a cart should be no different. Don't impede on your playing partners' sight lines, but lagging behind (even by a minute), all adds up and contributes to slow play.

If you do those things, you will have to work to play slowly. That's not to say that you have to be all golf, all the time. That can be exhausting. I have a buddy -- lets call him Carson -- who is one of the most laid back, kind-hearted people I know. Until you get him on the golf course. If he speaks thirty words the rest of the round, I'd be shocked. He plays golf like Patton approached battle. Don't get me wrong, dude can golf the ball, and that's great. But playing with him can be exhausting. He tells librarians that they need to shut up. If we were golfing in one of those Tibetan monasteries where they don't speak for years at a time, he wouldn't need to change his mannerisms a bit. They'd love him.

I have another buddy who's the exact opposite -- let's call him Andrew. Andy never stops doing anything not golf related. Maybe it's drinking one of the eleven beers he's going to down or checking his phone for the score of the game or texting his girlfriend about what they are doing that night. He's focused on his game for less than a total minute per round. He routinely has no idea where his ball is -- let alone where yours went, when you lost it looking in the sun.

I would implore you to try to find yourself somewhere in between those two playing styles. Golf is not a lifestyle, but you also didn't wander into a golf cart by accident. Pretend that you want to be there. Or don't. And stop playing.

Last thing, and this is a big one.

Playing through.

It's a lost art. It's all subtle nuance. It's a secret handshake, wrapped in an enigma, shrouded in secrecy.

I'm messing with you. It is the easiest thing in the world and very few people do it right. It's literally just allowing the group behind you to come play through, because they are ostensibly playing faster than you.

It doesn't mean they are better golfers than you. It doesn't mean they are better people than you. It doesn't mean that your group is a foursome of degenerates. No one is filing charges with a DA. It simply means that the people behind you seem to be playing faster than you, and you are trying to make a situation better in some way.

Here's how to make it work. First, identify that your group is actually the problem. If you are waiting on every tee box or in every fairway to hit, you aren't the problem. At that point, there's no point in letting anyone play through. I know, it's uncomfortable as the group behind you stands and waits, but if you are also standing and waiting. Allowing them to play through solves literally nothing. You'll end up waiting on them just as much as they have been waiting on you.

But if it's wide open in front of you, you should probably wave the folks behind you through. And be honest about the situation in front of you. If you are on the twelfth tee box and the last time you were waiting on the group in front of you was your approach to the second green, then you are not, in fact, in the proper position and you should let someone play through.

Now that you've identified that you are a problem group, there's three places to let them play through. One of them is much better than the other two.

The best place to do the swap is while you are on the tee box. It's a natural shift. Drive up, get out, without any clubs, and keep an eye on the group behind you. As soon as you see a cart get close to the previous green, make an exaggerated waving motion at them -- any group of golfers who has played before will recognize what you are doing. They'll likely putt out pretty quickly, and be out of your way in just a few minutes.

Don't do that thing where you tee off and then sit there, waiting for the group behind to drive up and then you tell them they can play through. You are only saving a few seconds and it makes the transition weird. Besides, if you tee off, the group behind you will hear the tee shots, and likely think you are not going to let them play through. Chances are, they'll just hang back a ways, to be polite. But if you are just standing near your cart (or on the box without clubs -- whichever gives you a better vantage point to see the group behind you), and you've waved at them to come up, they'll get the message. Exchange quick pleasantries, and let them tee it. Once they've driven away, you'll have a bit of a wait. Once they are out of the fairway, the tee box is yours again.

Keep in mind, if you are in the group getting waved through, this is the time to just hit a ball quickly and move on. The bigger audience doesn't mean it's time to workshop your comedy routine or look like a big guy and start a new bet with someone in your group. Just hit the balls and bail. Run free.

Another place you can do the swap is in the fairway of a par four or five. Hit your tee shots, drive up to them, hang out off to the side in the rough or trees, and wave the group behind up. This isn't as clean as the tee box because you have to wait for them to hit their drive and then their second shots. If anyone in that group has accuracy issues (or even distance disparity between themselves) it's a little weird. Also, it can make looking for balls harder, because there are likely to be eight to choose from, instead of only four.

The last place you can let someone play through is at the green. If you are on the green, and they are on the fairway, mark your balls, move off to the side, and wave them up. That should let them know what is going on and most players will do their best to wrap things up quickly.

This is the least ideal situation for two reasons. One -- if one of the players is having short game issues, it can take five to ten minutes to actually make this happen. Four players hitting tee shots and jumping into a cart should take less time. The other reason it's less than ideal is that you don't know what the other group's competitive makeup looks like.

By that I mean, are they in the middle of a huge match where every stroke and every hole counts? Then rushing them through the short game, of what may be a pivotal hole in the match, isn't great.

I know, it's far from the end of the world. But if you can do it the easy way or the hard way, you might as well take the easy way. Make the switch on the tee box.

That being said, letting someone play through at a less than ideal time is politer (my editor says that's a word and she knows her stuff) than not letting them play through at all. Letting faster groups play through encourages faster play, and that's never a bad thing.

One thing to note. If you have to let four groups or more play through you in the course of a round, then you have a problem. Maybe it's only one person in your group, or maybe it is several of you, but you need to address it. It shouldn't be up to the ranger to hand you your ass. You should be aware that you have a problem, and you need to address it for the good of the sport.

Again, it doesn't mean that anyone is a bad person. It simply means that they move too slowly on the course. If you need to give someone a copy of this book, with this chapter subtly highlighted, so be it. Hell, if you are giving someone a copy of this book to encourage them to play faster, get in touch with me through social media and I'll get you a discounted rate. Slow play is perhaps the most serious problem in golf today -- I know that means we've come a long way, considering at one point a man's skin color precluded him from playing a golf course at all -- but we can only fix this problem together.

Jeff Beck

The Head Game

Every sport is ninety percent mental. I know that now. I used to think golf was unique in that aspect, but it isn't. Playing quarterback, riding a mountain bike, or running marathons are all more mental than physical.

That said, golf is *really* mental. In part, because there's so much downtime between shots and so much flexibility within the game. I've literally seen someone stand over their ball, in the middle of the fairway, 150 yards from the green and pull their driver out, to effectively putt it the whole way. It was a downhill shot, super windy, and they thought it was their best bet.

They made par, so it certainly could have gone worse.

Part of what makes golf so great is also what makes it so frustrating. Without the other team guarding you, you can do whatever you want, which can often lead to overthinking a shot. You can put yourself into a vapor lock as you struggle to make a decision kicking around the pros and cons of your choice.

146

SUCK LESS AT GOLF

Having all the time in the world (or at least far more than the split-second the batter has when the pitch is on the way) doesn't help matters.

As hard as it might be, you need to turn off your brain. Overthinking things can only hurt you. If you stand over an approach shot, thinking to yourself "Don't put it in the bunker," there's a good chance it is going to end up in the bunker. Don't look at the sand. Don't think about the sand. The sand doesn't exist in your world. I know that's much easier said than done -- but it needs to be done.

There's a similar mindset in other sports. One of the first things you learn on a mountain bike is that you should only look where you want to ride. If there's a rock in the middle of a trail, look to the left or right of it, and you'll do just fine. If you look at that rock, you will hit it. Look at the NFL. The best cornerbacks track the quarterback's eyes, because many quarterbacks telegraph where the ball will be heading by staring at their receiver of choice.

On the flip side of "Don't think about what you don't want to have happen," having a clear mental picture of what you want to occur helps. I'm not advocating that you put together pictures and words on a poster board to help you capture your vision, en route to a supermodel wife and a pair of Ferraris in the garage. I'm advocating that you know what you want to have happen. And something as vague as "on the green" or "next to the pin" doesn't count.

How is that going to happen? Are you going to blade it into the bunker, hope it pops out and cuddles up to the pin? Are you going to aim ten yards left of the stick, knowing that your baby fade will move the ball toward the stick? Are you going to aim at the middle of green and hope the ball doesn't move? How are you going to get from where you are to where you want to be? I spent years just hitting the golf ball with the swing thought "Land it close" which is, for lack of a better word, stupid. It's retirement planning via scratcher tickets. Maybe it'll work out for somebody, but it isn't going with the highest probability option.

As for your shot, what does your normal shot look like? Do you play a little fade? Great, your new swing thought is _____ yards to the left of the pin, and fade it toward the hole. As amateur golfers, who are playing casually on courses that aren't set up to punish us, there is rarely no incentive for aiming anywhere but the pin. If a hole has water to the right of the green and the stick is on the right side, maybe add an extra three yards left to the spot where you are aiming, but don't let it change your life. It's a pond. It's likely not going to come into play. Don't run away from it or give this thing special treatment.

If you are the type of golfer who plays one course over and over, you can fall into a lull with club selection and how you play each hole. Maybe on the par-threes you vary your club selection, based on how far forward or back the pin is or what the wind is doing. In time you'll start seeing patterns based on your game. This can be both great and awful.

If you play a certain hole well a few times in a row, you're going to step up to the tee with some swagger in your stance. If you've been struggling to make bogey on it, you're going to tee a ball up with your tail between your legs.

There's a cliché in golf that I really enjoy. It sums things up very well. Sure, it sounds trite, but it's completely true.

There's only one shot that matters. This one.

It doesn't matter what you've done before. It doesn't matter what you will do in the future. Nothing has any influence over what you are about to do, except what you actually do. There's an argument to be made, that the last shot shaped this one. A cause and effect that means your bad drive put you into the rough or your good drive dropped you onto the fairway, but either way that's already happened. You cannot change it. That shot has set the stage for your next shot, so when you arrived on the scene, you knew what you were looking at. And if you are in the rough, who cares? It's slightly longer grass. Your playing partner doesn't get to park the cart right in front of you or use the butt of one of their clubs to knock your knee out of alignment when you are at the top of the swing. It's slightly longer grass, don't give it any more consideration than that. It doesn't have magic abilities.

As you go through your round, try to keep your "One shot at a time" philosophy going. For good rounds or bad ones, dwelling on the past gets you nothing. Riding a string of four straight pars doesn't make this next hole any easier. But thinking "I've never made five straight pars" can only make things harder. As you put pressure on yourself mentally, you hurt your game physically.

Being a goldfish on the golf course (at least for your memory of what happened in the past) wouldn't be the worst thing. As long as you can remember where your tee shot went.

Tangent time. There's a course in Northwest Phoenix, Coyote Lakes, that's short and narrow. It's not an executive course, it's still a par-71, but not a long 71. 360 yards and 440 yards are both par-fours, but one of them plays very differently than the other. Most of this course's par-fours are closer to 350 than anything starting with a four. In high school, I was playing this course for the umpteenth time with two good friends who didn't golf very often. At that point, they only dabbled in the game; they were too busy playing basketball, football, and having social lives to put much effort into golf. As a result, we didn't have any kind of bet going on and I didn't pay close attention to what I was scoring. I knew I was hitting the ball pretty decent, but nothing amazing.

We nearly had the course to ourselves and the round flew by. Driving away from the fourteenth green, I quickly added things up on my behalf. I'd made the turn with an even-par 36 and after making birdie on each of the par-fives on the backside, I was two-under. Which meant I was four incredibly easy pars away from shooting in the 60s.

At that point in my life, I had yet to shoot in the 70s. I was about to skip the 70s altogether and head right to the

60s. The world was mine. Yes, I was young and stupid.

The fifteenth hole was a relatively straightforward par-four. A little shorter than four hundred yards, I swung very smooth and controlled, and poked one right up the middle. I left myself about 140 to the stick. Perfect. The shot played out exactly as I wanted (if I'd put any thought into it beyond the "hit down the middle" swing-thought I was still desperately clinging to at that time). I was a smooth nine-iron away from making a two-putt par.

Unfortunately, the adrenaline in my system had other ideas. I was so jacked up, I swung with the unbridled ferocity that most cage fighters can't find until the later rounds of a match. That smooth nine-iron carried at least 170 yards.

After flying over the green by such a large margin, I didn't get up and down. But I saved bogey, and was on track to shoot under par -- still a hell of an achievement.

The sixteenth hole was a 160-yard par-three. I normally would have taken an eight-iron and stepped on it, or maybe just smooth a seven-iron. Fully aware of what had just happened, I opted for a smooth nine-iron, hoping that would be the right club, given the circumstances. Again, my ball sailed over the green. I didn't get up and down. Another bogey. Even par.

SUCK LESS AT GOLF

Seventeen and eighteen are both par-fours and both played the same way. Fine drive, took a ton off of the second shot, only to airmail the green in service of bogey.

I finished bogey-bogey-bogey-bogey to shoot a two over par 73.

It was my first time ever shooting in the 70s, and I was beaming, but internally I was furious. I wanted to snap every club over my knee, empty my bag into the parking lot, and then drive back and forth over the remains of my golf clubs until everything had broken some more.

My friends were amazed.

"Do you normally play that well?" one of them asked with wide eyes.

"No," was all I could muster. That was one of the most conflicted moments in my life. I was so happy for shooting a 73 and so angry that I dribbled a 69 off of my foot, I didn't know how to feel. I have no doubt in mind that if I hadn't added up my score, I'd have finished with a 68 or 69. But my brain got in the way, and that never ends well.

So if you don't want to do the math while you are playing, I'm all for it. If you can do the math and not focus on the score, then by all means, have at it. Everyone has to play their game their way, but you may want to consider ignoring the actual scoreboard, at least until the outside service guys are scrubbing your sticks. You may find that very little good comes from being aware of where you stand at any given moment.

Almost Never Say Never

I started working in golf for two reasons. First, I enjoyed the game and wanted to spend time around it. Secondly, I liked making people like golf. In the early 90's, TigerFever hadn't started yet and most people who liked golf were older than my dad. It wasn't an easy sell. In time, golf became more mainstream and that was fantastic.

Most golfers were ecstatic about their sport growing. More golfers meant more golf courses, more research and development going toward better golf clubs and balls, and better coverage of the PGA Tour.

Very few (literally zero golfers that I knew) thought, "Yeah, but there's going to be an influx of bad golfers I have to play with, through, or around."

However, most struggling golfers I've talked with over the years clam up at the thought of playing with better players. Most golfers (like most people in general) are actually pretty nice. Sure, we've all had stories of people being weird on the golf course (I've literally had death threats screamed at my group on the fairway, from somebody on the tee box who thought we were holding them up -- never mind the fact that the group in front of us was literally still visibly on the green of the par-four), but I think of those situations as a one-off. Maybe that guy got a cancer diagnosis the day before and needed to blow off steam. He was probably just having a bad day, not indicative of "golfers" as a whole.

The public-facing tee shot may be the new public speaking, in that it's golfer fear number one, but playing with a group of better golfers would be fear number two. That hasn't changed and it's not new. When I was selling golf clubs in 1996, I spent my work day with golfers who were trying to buy a better game.

"I don't need to be the best guy in my foursome, I just want to blend in with everyone else."

I can't tell you the number of times I heard that and, more than twenty years later, it's still alarming to think about -- especially since it came from adults.

There's a secret to playing with better golfers. With very few exceptions, most golfers aren't paying attention to you. Yes, they likely have an idea of where your ball went and who has the honor of hitting next, but they aren't living and dying on every one of your shots.

As long as you can play golf at a decent pace, most golfers really don't care how well you hit it. The legitimate scratch golfers (meaning by their handicap they shoot around par as a general rule) that I have played with over the years never complain about someone in the group playing poorly -- unless that player slowed down the group.

Most golfers get into a natural rhythm of things. If you throw off that rhythm and put bigger gaps than usual in between their shots, it can absolutely throw someone off of their game. For years, the Europeans have tried to do that (often successfully) in the big team competitions. Slow play as a weapon is a dick move, but when you are playing for the Ryder Cup, I get it. As a casual round, you want to avoid it completely.

This is why I'm a big fan of picking up your ball when all is lost. Now, doing so invalidates your score if you were going to post it for your handicap. If you maintain an official handicap, then you can ignore this whole chapter, and skip to the next one.

The other complication of picking up has to do with any type of bet you may have going. But odds are, if you are struggling bad enough that you are debating picking up, you've already lost the bet (though it gives credence to structuring more bets based on match play instead of stroke play -- that way, you can pick up and concede the hole and the match lives on). For the rest of you, it's all about drawing an arbitrary line and knowing that when you cross it, that hole is done and you're going to start fresh on the next tee box. Where you draw that line is up to you.

Maybe it's when you are lying double bogey, hitting triple bogey and you are still off the green -- maybe that's where you call it a hole and pick up. At that moment, nothing good is going to come from the hole and instead of spending several more minutes making a bad hole worse, you can tend the pin or even just hang out in the cart.

You are helping the course play faster.

I'm the last person to advocate cashing it in after only a bad shot or two. The best hole of golf I've ever played (or at least, the most head-shakingly *golf* hole I've ever played) was on the backside of the Meadow Course at Forest Highlands. It's a fairly lengthy par-five, and a good drive can either hit the lake on the left or get into the bunkers on the right. The lake traces the left side of the fairway all the way up to the green, and ends just short.

158

SUCK LESS AT GOLF

But a pond is in play on the right hand side, so there's water all over the place. Big risk, low reward, but it didn't keep me from swinging for the fences every single time I played it.

Fairly early on (when I still played a fade instead of a draw, so the lake wasn't a concern) I hit an okay drive, and had about two-hundred and eighty yards until I got to the green.

In my life, I've never hit a fairway wood two-eighty, much like, well just about anyone not playing golf professionally. That little fact didn't keep me from thinking that maybe this time it would happen. The added elevation kept my hopes alive (the higher you are, the thinner the air is and the further the ball carries -- estimates have put Flagstaff's 7,000 foot elevation as a ten to fifteen percent bonus). So I pulled my three-wood out of the bag, put my best John Daly imitation overswing on it, and hoped for the best.

I cold topped it. It went straight into the ground and popped straight up, probably about fifteen or twenty feet above my head. If I'd had been attentive, I could have ran underneath it, like an MLB catcher snatching a foul ball from an overzealous fan. The ball only went about 10 yards forward.

Which meant I, for my third shot, still had about two-seventy yards to go, and while I'd never hit a fairway wood two-seventy, that seemed more likely to happen than a second ago, when I needed two-eighty. Again I took a monster swing, only this time I made perfect contact, and absolutely pured it. It was the best swing of my life, with perfect timing and crisp contact. The ball took off like a rocket.

Unfortunately, it wasn't going at the green or even at the pond on the right. It was going well to the right of the pond, and ended up in the woods.

Eventually I found my ball, sitting on a little bed of pine needles, surrounded by trees. Exactly like I had planned. To my credit, it was pin high. Take that golf gods.

I had two options. Stab a wedge at it, in a backward fashion, hoping to clear the trees and the lake beyond that, to a spot on the fairway that would give me about a 40 yard pitch shot.

Or.

There was a gap about 14 inches wide, between two trees. In the middle of that gap was my view of the flagstick. Unfortunately, after the gap was a bit of rough, a lot of pond, a bit more of rough, and then a narrow

160

slice of green. Beyond the hole was another narrow slice of green, a tiny patch of rough, then bunker, then the cart path, and finally more native forest. The pin was all the way to the back of the green and, when you were approaching it from 90 degrees off the intended way, it was a very thin green.

Having literally nothing to lose, I put the ball back in my stance, took a little wedge swing, closed my eyes and punched it out.

Somehow, I hit that 14-inch gap like it was my job. The ball flew over the lake, landed in that tiny narrow spot of green, hopped once, and came to a stop less than a foot from the cup. I made a point of actually tapping it in for a legit par, instead of taking the gimme.

I'd made the single greatest par of my life, with a sub-standard drive, a horrific second shot, and a third shot that was forty degrees off of target line. If it wasn't for the punch shot, I would have up ended up making triple or quad-bogey. All it took was one great shot for redemption.

If a group had been waiting on us, I probably would've pocketed the ball in the woods, left to wonder forever what could have been. In reality, I'm sure I'd have never thought about it again. One of the many terrible holes I've played (and immediately forgotten about) in my life.

One of the many benefits of being an amateur golfer, is that nobody remembers your blow ups. Not like the professional ones. Not like:

Jean Van De Velde.

Do you remember that name? He was the guy who got to the 72nd hole of the British Open with such a commanding lead all he needed to do to secure his victory was make double bogey.

Then the wheels fell all the way off the wagon and he made triple bogey and lost in the ensuing playoff. Nearly two decades later and I still feel for the guy. We've all got some JVDV in us. We can ruin a surefire thing, but at least our mistakes aren't memorialized for all time.

Be ready to call a mistake a mistake, throw your ball in your pocket, and look forward to whatever the next hole is going to have in store for you. Just make sure that you have let that last hole go, and remember -- there's only one shot that matters. *This one.*

A Look Into The Bag

Golf bags are not meant to be lived out of. No, not even those massive cart bags. First and foremost, they exist to hold your clubs, a handful of balls and incidentals, and that's it.

If you can't carry your own golf bag, you need to start paring it down. Don't be that guy who shows up to the course, drives to the bag drop, pops the trunk, and lets the kid wreck his back collecting your 90-pound behemoth. This has nothing to do with being a better golfer, it is purely about being a better person.

I'm not saying you shouldn't use the bag drop. In fact, you should *absolutely* use the bag drop and let the guys do their work. But there's no way your bag should weigh much more than a small child.

If you need to keep fifteen to twenty balls in your bag because you normally lose at least one per hole, so be it. But that's the cap. No *more* than twenty balls and, if you have to have that many, you need to make sure you don't have $300 in change to act as ball marks as well. If you have more than a dollar in coins, you have too much in your bag. Pare it down. Tees don't weigh much (not nearly as much as coins) but just because you bought the 500 tee bag doesn't mean you should dump them into a pocket and be set for the rest of your life. Be an active participant in your hobby (and that means every now and then restocking your bag with the things that you'll need).

That's it -- I'm off my soap box. Now that we've established what you shouldn't fill your bag with, let's get into the specifics of what should go into your bag.

I hope, by now, that it is starting to sink in that you need to be honest with yourself. I mean truly honest with yourself, in order to make changes to your game. You have to acknowledge your weaknesses if you want to improve on them. If not, you are just going through the same motions over and over, expecting a different result. And that's crazy.

The biggest club-related mistake most people make is in their long irons. I get that. I literally did the same thing for a decade or more, and fought change tooth and nail.

Take a serious look at your set and your ability. What's the longest iron in your bag? I'm guessing there's a three or four-iron. If it is a two-iron, maybe you hit it well, and you are a long irons kind of player. Most of us aren't.

For argument's sake, let's say your longest iron is a three, because most iron sets come as a three-iron through pitching wedge. How well do you hit that club? How often do you hit it? How often do you stand over a ball sitting up perfectly in the fairway and think to yourself "I've got this"? Lastly, how often do you then hit the ball with that club and, in fact, "got this"?

If you are like most golfers, the answer to all of those are, "Not great, very rarely, almost never, and never", respectively.

You've got some dead weight in that bag. It's time to do something about it.

Hybrid clubs are a mix of woods and irons (hence the clever name). They have more loft than a standard fairway wood, but a slightly shorter shaft (both things make it easier to hit than a fairway wood), and a much lower center of gravity than an iron. In their infancy, they gained a reputation as being great for slower swinging female golfers and old men. Not sure where the marketing genius was on that one, but it only took a few years for us ego-driven guys to realize that, maybe it was worth putting one in the bag, so we could hit it two hundred to two-twenty with some semblance of control and accuracy.

Personally, once I tried one, I was hooked. I've hit shots with my hybrid that I couldn't dream about with an iron or a wood. Two-ten out, partially buried in a fairway bunker, with a nasty lip blocking the exit? An easy swing later, my next shot was a twelve-foot putt (which I promptly missed). The hybrid had enough loft to hit the ball high enough, before the lip could ruin the shot. It had enough height that, when the ball landed on the green, it ran out of steam instead of running off the back (which is what happened when I would hit my three-iron). Without my hybrid, I would have had to chop it out with a wedge, which would have left me with a partial wedge in. Not the end of the world by any stretch, but certainly a less than ideal situation. Especially since it can be avoided with a simple change of equipment.

Tour usage has fluctuated up and down with regards to hybrid usage. But again, modeling your game after the PGA Tour is a flawed model (rough estimates put PGA Tour usage somewhere between 30-65% of players -- a vast range). Meanwhile, the ladies of the LPGA use hybrids all the time. They don't all use them, but most do, simply because it allows them to hit better shots and play better golf.

SUCK LESS AT GOLF

I'm not advocating that you switch every iron to a hybrid (though if that's something you'd like, go for it, the option exists) and it isn't so straightforward that you can swap a three-iron out for a three-hybrid. I've found that equivalent-numbered hybrids will normally go farther than their matching iron. My first hybrid was a three and it went nearly twenty yards farther than my best-struck three-iron. That's not necessarily a bad thing, but it is worth keeping in mind if you are swapping irons out. Distance isn't king. Consistency is.

So now that we've gotten over that hurdle and we're all open to maybe putting a hybrid in our bag, we need to figure out what clubs in general we'd like to have in our bag.

Here's a list of the clubs that virtually all golfers will have in their bag, along with some sample yardages. Your distances will obviously vary, but should be somewhat similar.

Driver - 270 yards

Four-Iron - 195 yards

Five-Iron - 185 yards

Six-Iron - 175 yards

Seven-Iron - 165 yards

Eight-Iron - 155 yards

Nine-Iron - 145 yards

Pitching Wedge - 135 yards

Gap Wedge - 115 yards

Sand Wedge - 100 yards

Putter

That's eleven clubs, and leaves you three openings. Realistically, you should use at least two of those spots to fill the massive yardage gap between driver and four-iron. If you wanted to add a fourth wedge, I wouldn't fault you. Here's five common options to fill out the last three spots.

Three Wood - 240 yards

Five Wood - 225 yards

Three Hybrid - 220 yards

Four Hybrid - 210 yards

Lob Wedge - 80 yards

Personally I'd pick the three wood, three hybrid, and lob wedge. Having a two-forty club and a two-twenty club means two very different options when the shot calls for something longer than two hundred.

The lob wedge would rarely get hit as a full swing (I have a mental block about hitting a full swing shot sixty to eighty yards), but I'm a fan of the lob wedge for little touch shots around the green. Just pitch shots, none of that flop shot nonsense. I'm no flop shot elitist. I'm anti-flop shot for me as much as I am for you.

If you prefer to use all three options for longer shots, so be it. Ask yourself how many times a round you'll need a two-twenty-five club *and* a two-twenty club? I find I use my two-twenty club somewhere between once and four times per round (unless I'm trying something out and decide to tee off with it). I'm not sure that number goes up if I also have a two-twenty-five club. Odds are, I'm using each club once or twice, tops, which isn't a good use of the limited real estate in your golf bag.

I know I just outlined what may be a sizable investment of money, though I'm not trying to spend all of your money for you. Used clubs are perfectly fine to buy and at a fraction of the price of brand-new ones, you may want to explore that option. Allow me to give you some insight.

Golf Clubs

You don't have to buy the newest, latest, and greatest golf clubs. You can buy second-hand sticks, and you won't be worse off for it. You can buy used clubs and still be a member of the PTA, HOA, Mensa, or any other organization that'll have you. It doesn't make you a bad person.

However, you do need to draw the line somewhere. All used clubs are not the same. Used clubs and old clubs are very different. Used clubs are a few years from being the best technology. Old clubs are vintage and should be used for decoration.

Seriously.

Tangent time. My first year in the golf shop was fantastic. As the newest assistant pro on staff, I was at the bottom of the food chain when it came to day-to-day responsibility. I was in the shop though, so I had extensive playing and practice privileges. Whenever I was given the opportunity, I would go tee it up, frequently

170

with my buddy Joe (the guy who would lead the way out to Hawaii).

Joe was definitely the better golfer. He'd routinely beat me by a few strokes. As consistent as I was, he was just a little better. However, in driving distance, I had the advantage. I'd frequently outhit him by five or ten yards (just showing how little tee shots really matter to ones overall score), and he was okay with that. He was hitting a Callway Biggest Big Bertha (which at the time was every bit of ten years old, and it had some epoxy loose inside, so it made a jingling noise whenever he'd start his backswing) but true to Joe's character, he never once blamed his older club for any fault with his game.

He and I played together on a Wednesday afternoon, only to drop by the shop after we finished to check on something unrelated. The head pro handed Joe his new driver. Fresh from the factory, Joe had just leaped ten years forward in technology, with the latest and greatest from Ping. He looked it over, confirmed that the specs were exactly what he'd ordered, and he threw it in the bag.

The following afternoon, we were able to play together again. Joe proceeded to outdrive me on literally every hole, usually by twenty yards or more. It was a slaughter (though he still only beat me by a couple shots).

I was shocked. This was the biggest jump in equipment advantage I had (and still have) ever seen. I always knew that clubs could make a difference, but not to that extent. The more I thought about it, the more it made sense. I knew too many golfers that upgraded clubs on a regular basis, so the massive jumps forward got lost.

There was a lesson to be learned in this breakthrough. You are better off skipping multiple generations between club upgrades, in order to maximize your value. Golf club technology very rarely makes a quantum leap where they improve massively from one year to the next. The ads you might see online or in magazines will suggest as much, but marketing departments are infamous for using skewed numbers to represent their products in as favorable a light possible.

"The sweet spot is four times bigger than last year's model!" is a fallacy. The sweet spot, the true sweet spot, of a club is tiny, but the area of forgiveness (that's where you can hit the ball off-center and still get a pretty good shot) of a new model may grow by a small margin. In their quest to sell more golf clubs, manufacturers massage the numbers to make it look more impressive. When something goes from a two percent improvement to an eight percent improvement, they can tout FOUR

SUCK LESS AT GOLF

TIMES BETTER but, in reality, it's an improvement that can only be seen on paper. If you were to hit the two clubs back to back, you likely couldn't tell which one was "better."

Every couple of years, a golf club manufacturer will radically shift their direction with some revolutionary new technology breakthrough that's going to CHANGE THE GAME.

It usually isn't. And if it is, it'll stick around a while and everyone else will imitate it. You don't need to be the Alpha Consumer who tries every new club in an attempt to break through the invisible talent wall that your current club is holding you back from scaling. Largely because that scenario doesn't really exist at the amateur level. There's too much human error in the swing (which is why testing golf clubs with perfect swinging robots is cool and all -- but the biggest variable is the person holding onto the rubber end) so chasing theoretical variables isn't nearly as important as working on your short game.

In order to maximize your value, when looking at used clubs, I would recommend that you look at clubs that are less than four years old. Clubs that are only one year old are ideal, since they should be only a fraction of the cost of the latest and greatest. Think about it objectively. At some point in the last twelve months, these clubs were among the pinnacle of golf club engineering. Think about what's happened in the last year. How fast it's gone by -- and the clubs you are looking at for less than half of retail were the exact clubs that marketing campaigns were fawning over. Trust me, those sticks are still great.

But so are the clubs that are two to four years old. The hardest part about buying four-year-old clubs is finding a set that isn't beat to hell. That said, they do exist. There are tons of golfers out there who, for whatever reason, take time away from the game and, when they return, want to upgrade (after all they've taken three years off the game and THE GAME HAS CHANGED multiple times in their absence, and they need to catch up), and you can swoop in and get a deal.

One thing to keep in mind -- wedge and iron technology has not progressed at nearly the rate that wood and hybrid tech has. Five-year-old irons, given that they are in good shape, can still be amazing -- and instead of paying $800 at retail for a brand new set, you can routinely find an older set for less than $200. Working in the industry, it wasn't uncommon to see guys rocking several decade old Ping irons along with a new set of woods every nine months.

The most important thing to look for when you're trying to find a new set of irons, isn't how new the technology is, but to make sure it's the right club for you.

Allow me to explain.

Drivers spent decades around the same size, then someone realized that a bigger club could be more forgiving, and the driver market blew up. In a very short time, we went from thinking a 190 cc club was oversized, to 250 cc, to 320 cc, to 360 cc -- the line just kept moving. Fairway woods were going up in size too, but they could only go so far. Since a driver is meant to be hit off of a tee exclusively (you golfers who hit driver off the deck are weirdos, there, I said what we're all thinking), they could make them impossibly large. You couldn't do that with a fairway wood, because when one would get too large it would be unwieldy out on the course. But driver sizes just kept growing and we started seeing club failure rates. Parts of the club head would literally dent or just shear simply on impact as the head grew and the material kept getting stretched thinner and thinner.

At a certain point, the USGA weighed in, and decided that 460 cc was the biggest a driver club head could be the arms race ended. However, manufacturers had already made clubs much larger, and had been tinkering with variable thicknesses of the heads. In doing so, they learned that they could create something of a springboard effect to the face. That led to a whole new rule regarding COR (Coefficient of Restitution) which measured how much a club face flexed back before it exploded, launching the ball artificially long.

I can't tell you how much fun it was to work in golf as that was happening. Fights over which drivers were legal, which led to furious people discovering that their relatively new driver had been ruled illegal for play sometime after they purchased it. Good times.

To find your driver, find something that fits for you for flex and loft (good rule of thumb -- don't go under eight degrees of loft unless you can hit your five iron one-ninety to two-hundred yards), and then least importantly, find something you like to look at. There's so much "design" pumped into these things, some can look like an exotic European super car. And that's fine if that's what you like, but if you don't like the way it looks, it won't end well for you. For a little while, Cleveland Golf (who make some amazing wedges) was putting out a series of woods that looked slightly like a high school art student's project ashtray. They had a sculpted down back edge and, while they hit the ball a very long way, they looked odd, had a strange feel and an alien sound at contact. Unless you were into all of that (and a number of golfers were) it was hard to recommend someone hit that driver. So find what you like to look at, because that truly does matter.

Regarding your irons -- you need to play appropriate clubs. No one reading this book should entertain the thought of playing blades. Period. No exceptions. I literally have a set of blades in my garage that I got for a song, years ago. I've hit them exactly once at the range and I didn't swing anything below a six-iron -- even though the eBayed set came with every club from the pitching wedge down to the one-iron. Part of me would love to meet the psycho who thought, "Yeah, I should totally put a one-iron in my bag, since they're BLADES."

If you don't know what a blade is, picture a golf club from eighty years ago. Something with a flat back (which is why they are sometimes called muscle-backs) instead of a cavity, and that's a blade. They are still made today in limited quantities and there have been improvements, but they don't offer enough performance for the average golfer -- especially in light of what modern clubs do offer: the area of forgiveness.

Years ago, they started testing with robots to test golf

clubs and their "sweet spot," which is the single, best place on the club face you can hit the ball. On irons, you want it fairly low on the face (same with fairway woods and hybrids) and on a driver, you want it relatively high on the face. But one thing became quickly apparent -- the "sweet spot" was really small on every single club. Smaller-than-a-pea level of small. While cavity-back irons had the same tiny sweet spot, they did introduce a substantial amount of club face square footage that fell into the "area of forgiveness," which is where you can still hit off of perfect and get a relatively decent shot. Everything is energy. Hitting a golf ball is simply energy transfer and the sweet spot is where the most energy was imparted on the ball -- the science is hazy, but for argument's sake, let's just say that a perfect shot transfers ninety percent of the energy in a swing to the ball. The area of forgiveness of an oversized cavity back club would still transfer eighty to eighty-five percent of that energy. In the grand scheme of things, not a huge loss from the sweet spot. At the same time, blades had the same-sized sweet spot, but only a minuscule area of forgiveness. If you missed your shot by more than a hair or two, you were only getting forty to fifty percent of energy transfer -- which meant a very bad shot.

That doesn't mean much for great golfers. They are going to hit within that small area of forgiveness 99.99999 percent of the time, and they aren't going to lose sleep over the .00001 failure rate. They also approach the ball with the confidence that they can make it do what they want. In addition to being a much smaller head, without perimeter weighting, blades tend to have very little offset. Offset is the small measurement of the space between the leading edge of the hosel (which is where the shaft goes into the head) and the leading edge of the club face. Offset is commonplace on oversized clubs and having an offset club effectively gives you an extra few milliseconds to square up your club face at impact. It also means extra difficulty, if you want to hit a draw that goes *that* much left to right, versus a draw that goes *that* much left to right (when you read that, read the second *that* with even more emphasis). They are designed for the golfer who has complete control of their game and has a swing thought like "I'm going to hit a four-yard fade -- this eight-iron is going to travel 160 yards, and in that time, it will fade four yards from left to right," (Side note: no golfer in the world has ever had that swing thought, but I am just making a point).

In addition, blades are typically forged instead of cast,

which makes for a softer club head. That doesn't change much on the performance side of things, but it does help club feel. You can hit a cast club well and have it still feel rough, but when you hit a forged club well, you will know it. It almost doesn't feel like you hit it. The impact disappears. However, a few decades ago they started forging some cavity-back irons as well, so if you want to spend a little extra money, you may want to look in that direction. Most forged cavity-backs are a little smaller, have less offset, and are altogether less forgiving, so if you are struggling to break 100, maybe put those off for now too.

The best analogy I've ever heard, to compare a blade and a cavity-back iron -- it's like hitting a ball with a tennis racket and then hitting the same ball with a two-by-four. The tennis racket will feel pretty good and go pretty well, as long as you hit it in the strings. It's going to be fine. The two-by-four has one or two spots where the ball is going to do what you want, but the rest of it is going to be a bad experience. The ball isn't going to go where you want, and it's going to hurt like hell. Hitting a blade poorly literally stings your hands, like if you were to hit something with a two-by-four.

We have ruled out blades, which is helpful, but what

should you be looking at? First, you don't have to stick with major brands (Callaway, Taylormade, Cleveland, etc), but you might as well. They tend to use mass-produced and readily available components (like shafts that are sold in golf shops, instead of something made in house that might be of a lesser quality). I would recommend most golfers stick with steel shafts of some sort for their irons. However, if you have hand pain or arthritis issues, you might find the extra cost of graphite shafts worth it for the vibration dampening, if nothing else. Most golfers will not see much performance enhancement from graphite shafts (at least in their irons) but if that's what you want to play with, have at it. Just expect to pay a little more. There's also a higher chance that something can go wrong with the shafts as they age. Unprotected areas of a golf bag can rub against the shaft and eventually break through the outer layer. Once the outer layer has been compromised, it is an eventuality that the shaft will break. Having a shaft replaced isn't major surgery, but it is an inconvenience and additional cost.

You can roll the dice and look on your local Craigslist or eBay, but there are better options out there. GlobalGolf.com and 2ndswing.com (I have no affiliation of any type with either company) both have a great reputation and there's a level of confidence you get from buying from a business, instead of some guy whose clubs belonged to a little old lady, who only drove them to church once a week. You may end up paying a little more, but by and large, their prices appear to be roughly in line with private sellers. I spent some time piecing together full sets of clubs to replace my own (driver, three-wood, three-hybrid, four-iron through wedge, gap wedge, sand wedge, lob wedge, putter) and found a number of ways to do so for less than $800 shipped.

Yes, $800 is a lot of money. But, a few years ago what I put in the cart would have been closer to $3500 and (minus a few cosmetic blemishes) those clubs will perform just as well as they were when they were new. They aren't iPhones. The manufacturer cannot make the old ones worse with age. You certainly don't *need* to buy any new (or new to you) clubs. That exercise was to show that if you did *need* to replace your whole set (lost in fire, stolen, or accidentally thrown into a lake after a particularly bad day) you could.

As long as you have fairly modern golf clubs that fit your ability level, you are far better off spending money on lessons and range time than you are on club upgrades. A seven percent more forgiving driver doesn't mean you are going to hit seven percent more fairways or hit the ball seven percent farther. It means that, when tested with a robot, there was a certain spot on the face where seven percent more energy was transferred to the ball -- that's it. Marketing is a hell of a drug.

The only place you can disregard all of this, is putters. It isn't a bad idea to have at least two putters that you switch between and if you end up with three or four, so be it. I've heard people claim that their "putter ran out of good putts" but that's not what I'm talking about. I'm not talking about rocking one of those long putters or belly putters either (bad ideas both, just learn how to putt the right way and you won't have people mocking you behind your back) so much as having completely different looking club heads. Listen, it's a putting stroke -- not that much can go wrong during the motion. You pivot your shoulders back and forth, with minimal hip movement, and very little wrist in the action -- all you're doing is sweeping the kitchen floor. Technology doesn't make putts, good reads and solid fundamentals do.

There is, however, a growing movement within the last few years with the idea that there is a certain putter type for each person. That you should get personally fit by someone trained in the fine arts of putter divining, and that a face-balanced or offset putter to your exact specifications will mean more putts made. Not to sound like an old-man skeptic, but okay, maybe. It certainly can't hurt and, even if it is just placebo effect, so be it. If doing that gives you more confidence that you will make a putt, than you may want to look into it. For me, I look at the simplicity of the putting stroke and realize that bad alignments and bad reads make up the vast majority of missed putts. Not poorly struck balls. Especially since a slight change in the offset of a putter isn't going to fix every miss-struck putt -- we're talking percentage points. Knowing that the process can be very pricey, I think there are much better ways to spend your money, if you want to putt better. And none of them involve giving money to me -- whereas, most of the people I see advocating for putter fitting are the people who fit putters.

Having the same driver for two or three years, or the same set of irons for a decade, is good. It's familiar. In time, you will know what you like and dislike about those clubs. With a putter, it's more precise. Everything matters more. And I have found that, even when I was putting well, swapping what flat stick was in the bag every few months kept me putting well. Have a wide variation -- the Ping Anser (which is also the same design as a Scotty

SUCK LESS AT GOLF

Cameron Newport, or an Odyssey #1, or probably forty other putters that are virtually identical) is a good putter to keep around, along with some form of mallet putter, and maybe something that's center-shafted. The center-shafted type (I still use a Ping iSeries 1/2 Craz-E, which has been discontinued but you can find online pretty easily) is nice because you have to really mishit it to get a bad roll. The shaft goes into the club at or near the center of the club head (hence the cryptic name), so it resists twisting. But putters are a personal preference. There are more expensive putters out there than ever before, but that doesn't mean that a twenty-dollar putter is bad. The best putter is the one that you like and that you feel confident in. Don't overthink it, especially when it comes to "new technologies" with special inserts or gimmicks. Yes, an insert can make a putter feel "better" but there have been so many weird "what the hell were they thinking" putters that have aged poorly.

Anyone remember the Taylormade putter whose face resembled a basketball? Something about the bumps on it were supposed to give it a truer roll. Or the Teardrop putter, whose entire face was radiused in a way to only give good contact reduce any kind of skidding? They were also the ones who kept pointing out that other putters made putts skid, and not roll. Cue the eye roll.

Top Flite spent half a decade putting grooves on the faces of their putters and a number of others tinkered with exotic metals to get "extreme weight balancing" to make your putters sweet spot better. As if the putting stroke were not a simple back and through.

It worked though. I have seen too many of those clubs riding on the back of golf carts for it not to have been a successful marketing campaign.

Spend time looking at putters -- find one you like to look at and you have some modicum of confidence in. From there, tap a few balls with it. If you like the way it looks and feels (both in your hands as well as at the point of impact), then great, you've found a putter. If not, keep looking.

You can go down the rabbit hole of matching your set, having a full bag filled with nothing but one brand, but it's not necessary. I prefer to keep my wedges the same (or at least my gap/sand/lob wedge) so they are from the same family. That helps keep things consistent, both in appearances, as well as little things like lie and shaft length. You should be able to pick your loft, but lie and length are usually outside of your control. I've gone the route where my fairway wood and driver were made by the same manufacturer and I've gone the other way -- that's pure cosmetic preference. But having homogenous wedges will never hurt you.

Your wedges are the one place I would advocate buying new. Not buying new every year, but maybe every few years -- and the reason isn't what you are thinking.

If you've ever seen an ad for a wedge (or had a conversation about wedges) odds are that it focused on the *grooves*. Those magical little canals that give spin to some and keep it from others, at a seemingly arbitrary rate. Well, sadly, that ain't it.

Grooves play a part in imparting backspin on the ball, but there are golfers out there than can hit a sand wedge, have the ball hop once and zip backward with a thirty-year-old club. I've seen people take groove-less golf clubs and knock it stiff. The fact is grooves are primarily there in order to keep water droplets and debris off of the impact surface of the club. That's it. Yes, fresh grooves on a wedge can bite into a softer golf ball. That doesn't mean that it's generating spin -- spin is all predicated on the impact. I'm not going to give a class on how to hit a shot with backspin (I already covered that in the opening chapter of my first novel, *Outside Service* -- if you haven't read it yet, you should give it a shot), but I always like to think of it like putting English on a cue ball in billiards. You can't just hit it where you want, you have to clip it just right.

The reason you should entertain buying new wedges is all because of loft and lie (but mostly the lie). Every golfer knows what loft is, but lie is also crucially important, primarily in your shorter clubs. Lie is the angle between the shaft and the ground when the golf club is sitting squarely on the ground. What you see when you set the club on the ground, and what happens when you take a swing can be two different things. All of this is why you should have your lie checked, and if it is very far off you should look into getting your clubs professionally bent for you. This can be very hard to do with older sets of clubs or with cast iron (forged irons bend far easier). While lie is important for all of your irons, the added loft of your wedges will exacerbate any lie deficiencies that your clubs might have. If we were standing in the same room, I could make a demonstration that shows that a four-iron's resulting path of a golf ball does not change much if the lie is off even as much as four degrees either upright or flat, but two degrees off for a sand wedge could be the difference between hitting the green and missing it altogether.

SUCK LESS AT GOLF

I know what you're saying. "But Jeff, I've had my lie checked, and I'm pretty much standard." Cool. Me too. Most of us are, that's why the standards are what they are. They fit most people. But what lie that five-year-old wedge was shipped with, and what lie it has today is not always the same thing.

Wedges are typically made of a little softer steel. It gives better "feel" and "more touch around the green." I put those in quotes, because there's an argument to be made that they are less about marketing and more about real world consequence (and there's also a powerful counter argument). Regardless, softer metal means that they can be bent easier. Like that time you chunked your pitch shot and then slammed the club down in anger. Or maybe that time you chipped it in, then whipped the club back toward your golf cart so you didn't have to carry it while you tended to the flagstick for your friends. Also, keep in mind, your wedges will likely be your most used clubs. When you add all of that up, there's a decent chance that your five-year-old wedges lies have changed since you got them.

It doesn't hurt that wedges are typically the least expensive clubs in the bag. A top level wedge, made by any of the best brand names, can be had for about $100.

If you want to opt for a different finish, that number can hit $150, but you can also find them on sale for as low as $70-80. And you don't have to buy three. Spending $150-200 on a new gap wedge and sand wedge will likely have a much greater effect than putting that money toward a new driver. Even if they don't help you spin the ball backward.

Besides -- that's as much the ball's fault as anything else.

Golf Balls

When I was in high school, I had to go to the hospital because I cut open a golf ball.

It wasn't the first golf ball I'd ever cut open. I'd cut open dozens of them -- I don't know why, I mean, as a golf-nerd-kid I liked to collect the cores of the ball, but to be honest, you could probably chalk it up to video games just not being very good back then. I could cut open just about any type of ball. The ball of choice would be some sort of balata or even a Titleist Professional (the precursor to today's ProV1), once they got scuffed up enough. It wasn't that long ago that golf balls were fragile little spheres, perfect in their packaging, just waiting for the world to scuff them.

The day I went to the hospital, I had grabbed a knife from my brother's room (I would later learn it was his sharpest one as he'd spent hours honing the blade to a virtual laser beam) and I went to town carving up the ball. The Titleist Tour Balata cover could be torn by a particularly insistent fingernail, so you can imagine what happened when I took the small equivalent of a katana to one.

I slipped slightly, and at first, I thought I had punctured the core. During that era, high spinning golf balls used literally liquid filled rubber cores surrounded by tightly wound-up rubber bands, and I figured I had somehow punctured the core. A moment later, I realized that was actually my blood that was shooting all over the place. The knife was so sharp it went right to the bone and while I'm no hero when it comes to pain, it didn't hurt at all. My friend Nick was in the room at the time and he's always been one of those, "Sorry your leg got caught in the blender, but hey, at least you have another one so let's go ride bikes" kind of a guy. The shooting blood unnerved him, and he ran to get my mom. Hours later, after going into shock in the hospital from all of the lost blood, I returned home with a newfound respect for my brother's knife collection, and a bunch of stitches in my thumb. By that point there was a pool of dried blood on my awesome blue carpet (80s carpet was the best) with actual blood spatter on the wall more than six feet away from where I was when the accident happened.

I'd like to say, that this incident is what got me to stop

cutting golf balls open, but really it was more the fundamental change in golf ball construction that came shortly thereafter that killed my side hobby. Balls didn't get noticeably harder, but they got much harder to cut into. The balls no longer had a liquid-filled core, surrounded by rubber bands that would spit all over the place as you peeled the cover open.

This is a good thing. And not just to keep the rest of my fingers intact and free of scars. The new generation of golf balls are a quantum leap forward from a few decades ago.

There are so many good golf balls on the market today, you almost cannot make a bad choice. There was a time that every single golfer on Tour played Titleist (even guys rocking a MaxFli visor were usually playing Titleist balls) and any amateur golfer worth his salt played Titleist too.

No longer.

That isn't to say that Titleist doesn't still make a good ball. It does. But so does virtually everyone else, at almost every performance level and price point.

Bridgestone, Callaway, Nike, Srixon, Taylormade and a number of others, all make a damn fine golf ball. Some people see that as a problem, because they can't figure out what they should use.

Yeah, having too many good options is a real head scratcher. The kind of thing that keeps you up late at night.

Here's how to figure out what ball is going to be *your* ball.

That's right, you are looking for one (and only one) and that's going to be the one you use. Not out of some brand loyalty thing (don't get a Srixon tattoo on your biceps or anywhere else -- that's just weird. Unless they are paying you obscene amounts of money, then go for it) but because golf is all about consistency and repeatability. Hitting a seven-iron 200 yards is great if you were planning on it, but when you didn't want to hit it that far you just ruined your round. Not that there's any ball on the market that can make *that* happen, but you should stack the deck in your favor as much as possible. It is important to keep as few variables from shifting (which is the same reason I advocate buying your tees instead of hoarding them from the golf carts at the courses you play -- always using the same length of tee is a good thing). Is that convincing enough? Are you on board with the fact that you only need to find one ball? Great, now onto the how. If not, read through that last paragraph again, and then catch up with the rest of the class.

First and foremost, take a look at your budget. Is spending $40-50 per dozen balls in the cards for you? No? Okay, no worries at all. Stepping down from the top-tier ball no longer means making huge sacrifices, like it used to. You can still get a ball with plenty of spin, durability and softness, without playing the same ball the folks on Tour do. These sell for twenty-something per dozen -- and that's a non-sale price too.

To a certain degree, now is the time to completely disregard everything you have read about golf balls. It's weird, for as good as golf balls are, every brand is falling over themselves to tell you tall tales about what their ball can do. No ball can leap over tall buildings in a single bound or cure cancer, but we're only a few months away from seeing those as bullet points.

The number of dimples on a golf ball don't matter to you. Nor does anything about "a penetrating ball flight" or "exotic core." What matters to you is how the ball plays. And you can't figure that out, without playing it a bit. There are a few things you can look at ahead of time to help narrow the field of prospective balls.

Cover. If it is urethane, that's great, but probably outside of the twenty-something per dozen budget. You may be able to find a urethane cover ball in that range on an occasional deal, but that means if you can't find a deal, you'll be spending much more money, or finding a new ball.

Most budget conscious balls are covered with a different synthetic material, surlyn. However, not all surlyn balls are created equal. For a while, surlyn balls were thought of poorly, but now there are a number of good choices. Feel is a big part of telling the good ones from the bad ones, so you will see many golfers open a sleeve of balls, and pull one out. Then they will run their thumbnail against the surface of the ball, as if they were trying to cut into it. First, it ain't going to happen (and secondly, if you did manage to cut it -- not cool, unless you were going to buy the damaged ball), but mostly WHY ARE YOU DOING THAT?

Your thumbnail doesn't feel nearly as well as your thumb and/or forefinger. You should hold the ball and get a feel for it -- a softer cover will feel slightly different than the rock-hard Top Flite XL balls of yore and they will feel better on every shot, including the putter.

This is an in-person type of thing. When you are trying to find your ball, don't shop online.

The other thing to look into, besides cover, is spin. I

touched on this earlier -- there isn't a golf ball in the world that will magically make your six-iron zip back, but there is such a thing as a high-spin or low-spin golf ball. It isn't nearly as important for most golfers in the backspin department as much as it is the sidespin department.

If your normal ball flight moves left-to-right (and roughly eighty to ninety percent of all golfers hit the ball that way), then, as we discussed earlier, you are somewhere between the fade and the slice. If you only fade it, then you should play a ball that claims to have a higher spin rate. Spin is good, provided that you can control it. If you find yourself in a lifelong battle with a slice, then you should target a ball that claims to have a lower spin rate. They may also market these balls as STRAIGHT DISTANCE. STRAIGHT DISTANCE is a huge stretch (if you were going to hit a massive slice then you are still going to slice it) but it can keep from making it worse.

Let me give you a few specific examples of balls to choose from. This is accurate in mid-2017, but things may have changed (depending on when you are reading this.)

I'm a fan of Bridgestone, not just because they make a great tire (and they do) or because they've ever given me anything for free (they haven't) but because they've made a number of second and third tier balls that are damn good. When I stopped working in the golf industry, I also lost the ability to buy golf balls cheaply (or simply be given a dozen every now and then with the words STAFF written on the side -- that was a really cool perk). So I went in search of a good golf ball that didn't make me visibly angry at the cashier when I swiped my card.

Bridgestone's top-level ball is the B330 and B330-S. Both are played on various Tours all over the world. The only difference between them is that one of them is the higher club head speed variant (kind of the difference between the ProV1 and ProV1x) but that doesn't really affect us in this conversation. They are usually about $45 per dozen, and I'm out on that. They also have the B330-RX and B330-RXS, but those are still $40/dozen, and too pricey.

I've been a fan of the e6+, but that ball has disappeared and split into several similar but different balls; the Bridgestone e6 Speed, the Bridgestone e6 Soft, and the Bridgestone e6 Straight Flight. You can routinely find either ball for $28 per dozen (as low as $20 per dozen if you know how to type the word "sale" into the search window) and it's a great ball. The Soft will give you more spin, the Speed will give you less spin, and the Straight Flight won't fill you up and never lets you dow-- nope, that's Bud Light's slogan from twenty-five years ago. I couldn't tell you what the real-world differences are between the Speed and the Straight Flight are. Perhaps the Soft is the high spin, Speed is medium spin, and Straight Flight is low spin, but at the end of the day, you still have to hit the ball and figure out what works for you.

I can tell you, they all have a reasonably soft cover. Not the kind that you would cut through en route to the hospital, but also not the kind to make an almost metallic click, as you hit it with your putter.

Bridgestone also has the e5 and the e7 to add to the confusion. One of them is all about its "high trajectory" versus its sibling's buzzword "piercing trajectory."

I'm not saying you shouldn't try them, just that you shouldn't read the marketing materials. If you are iffy, don't grab a full dozen, just a sleeve or two. Start on the putting green, because if a ball feels bad off of the putter, literally nothing else matters. You should work backward and, instead of finding *your* ball, you can work through the lineup of everything that isn't *your* ball.

Bridgestone also has the TreoSoft (I don't know what that word means) and the Extra Soft (I know what that means) golf balls that start at $21 per dozen and go down from there. That may mean that they are a lesser ball, or manufactured somewhere where tariffs don't add to the cost. We may never know.

Below is a general list of balls, by manufacturer that you may want to try out. It's far from a complete list, and varying manufacturers different verbiage can be confusing, but based on my experience, these balls could easily find their way into your bag.

Bridgestone

e6 Speed, e6 Soft, e6 Straight Flight, e5, e7, TreoSoft, Extra Soft

Callaway

Diablo Tour, Speed Regime (which are based on your swing speed -- likely you want the Speed Regime 1 or 2), SuperHot 55/70, Supersoft

Nike

RZN Speed White, RZN Speed Red, Hyperflight

Srixon

Tri-Speed Tour

SUCK LESS AT GOLF

TaylorMade

Penta, Penta Speed, RocketBallz Speed (which is a terrible name for a good ball), RBZ Distance

Titleist

Velocity

Top Flite

Gamer Tour, Gamer Soft

Last thing on golf balls. You may have seen high numbers (which are usually numbered five through eight, instead of the usual one through four -- some people prefer that for whatever reason, personal idiosyncrasy or they just like being different), which are legal for play, and X-outs, which are not.

X-outs aren't legal for play for kind of a stupid reason. For years, there's been spot checks on golf balls -- they can't go too far under a specific set of tests with a robot. If they did, they were labelled illegal, and the company that made them would cross out the name (hence the phrase X-out) and sell them for range or general practice use. That doesn't really happen anymore but they still sell X-outs that are the result of a visual blemish. Yes, you can save money on them and maybe play a more expensive ball, but don't do it. Don't play an illegal ball, even if you aren't the handicap-tracking type. Eventually you'll play with someone who throws a fit over it, and while he's kind of in the wrong for his way of approaching it, he's not completely in the wrong, since your ball is illegal. There's plenty of good legal balls waiting for you. Go find yours.

SUCK LESS AT GOLF

How To Be Everyone's Favorite Member

If you are a regular member at a golf club, or you play the same course all the time and nobody knows your name (without looking at your personalized bag tag) then this chapter is for you.

Or maybe not. Maybe you don't want people to know you (be it a stipulation of your witness relocation program or you claim that you don't need other's approval to be happy). However, most people enjoy being liked by other people. And this is all about having people around the course like you.

As with most things, there's an easy way -- money. If you tip well, you will find yourself on everyones good side. It doesn't need to be obscenely well, but if you wrap up your day and hand the kid scrubbing your sticks a ten or twenty to put into the pot, they will remember you. The fifth time you do it, guys who you've never seen will know your name. You've been solidified as a good tipper. And everyone knows the good tippers.

The first habitually good tipper I met was a longtime member at FH named Dave Kitchens. He'd throw a twenty every time he played (unless he played with his wife, and then he'd probably throw two twenties). He was from Vegas -- a city that understands tipping better than all of Europe combined and he was well loved by the staff. Though, part of that was he was one of the most genuine members we had too.

Dave, or after you'd met him a few times, Kitch (at a course where all other members were formerly addressed as Mr. _____, Mrs. ____, or Dr. ____), knew just how much to push everyone's buttons, but in a friendly manner. If there was a guy who was hung over, he'd make fun of him. If someone didn't know how to iron his own slacks, Kitch would mention it. But then he'd grin in a "Yeah, but I'm really hungover and I'm shitty with an iron too," kind of way, which made the guy getting mocked like Kitch even more.

Not many people can make friends by insulting them (and it wasn't just the forthcoming twenty that made it okay). If you aren't charming (and you know if you aren't) then maybe don't make personal attacks at the expense of the staff. Stick with being a decent tipper.

Another favorite member of the staff was Mr. Burt

SUCK LESS AT GOLF

Turney. Mr. Turney might be the most genuinely nice person on the planet. And the fact that his golf swing was pure butter didn't hurt either. He wasn't a huge tipper (a few bucks each time) but that didn't matter. When he asked you how your day was going, he kept looking at you until you answered and he genuinely wanted to know the answer. If it wasn't going well, he wanted to make it better. I never learned what Mr. Turney did before he retired and started playing really good golf at least five times per week (frequently with Roe McBurnett -- what I'd give to be a regular member of that group), but I would be surprised if his co-workers and employees didn't love him.

What's more, I have no doubt whatsoever, that if I told any of this to Mr. Turney, he'd be shocked. Treating people well wasn't his way to ingratiate himself to the employees, it was literally just every day for him. And not just the head pro. The new kid just working for the summer in the locker room shining shoes was treated just as well as the general manager.

Which is something that you should keep in mind. Much like the guy who makes his date uncomfortable by treating her well and then being incredibly rude to the waiter, treating the head pro and the rest of the management well, then treating the outside service staff with disdain will only end poorly for you. You don't need to take the guys out drinking (though it doesn't hurt -- HINT HINT) or adopt anybody into your home and pay for college. Simply treating the outside staff like they are someone you like (or someone you like's son or daughter) is more than enough to get put on the informal but non-existent good list.

Why should you care?

If you play at a private club or you are a regular at a public course, being well-liked has benefits and opens doors that you didn't know existed. Last second cancellation, three spots before your tee time? If the starter likes you, you will be the first person he approaches, to see if you'd like to take the newly vacant spot. Or maybe the guy in the golf shop charges your guest the "family guest" rate, even though your guest's last name is very different from yours. If your club offers valet parking, your car (regardless of what you drive) will be readily available, usually with the clubs waiting in the trunk. Golf course employees are trained to anticipate the needs of all players, but they go very far out of their way to make absolutely certain that the members that they like have a much better experience.

SUCK LESS AT GOLF

One thing that most golfers don't realize is that they should let the staff do their job. Utilize the bag drop. Have them clean your clubs and have your clubs waiting for you at the bag drop after the round. Every course has its own method of doing things and if you dig in your heels to do it *your* way, you will throw a wrench into that system. Even if you think you are helping, you are not. For example, instead of letting the guys clean your clubs and set them at the drop to wait for your inevitable exit, you do that thing where you drive the cart back to the clubhouse, unclip your bag and hurriedly walk out to the parking lot, while the rest of your group looks on dismayed. Sure, you saved yourself a few bucks for the guy not to clean your clubs, or the embarrassment of not throwing a tip after the kid has cleaned your clubs. What you are missing is that tips are pooled together and split up after the fact. Everyone who's done their job to make your day better gets a piece of that one to two dollars you didn't throw into the pot. But more importantly, when the head pro sees you walking with your own bag out to the lot, he going to chew out whoever is working at the bag drop for allowing you to do so. The head pro doesn't care that you waved the kid off and said you were good -- every other golfer that you are going to walk past in the parking lot doesn't know that you were being obstinate. To the head pro, every other guest that sees you walking with your sticks slung over your shoulder is going to think that his staff did a bad job. Let the employees do their job. It doesn't matter if you are a member or a guest, in many ways, if you are a golfer, then you are a guest at the course. The golf course will be very accommodating to you, but there are certain things you need to do to make it easier on them. Using the bag drop is one of them.

I touched on this slightly in my novel, *Outside Service* (which was 99% fiction but this part was based on fact), but there were a number of members who liked certain things certain ways. If you are nice, it is far more likely that, if you are one of those people, you will get your way. And as a member or repeat guest, the best thing you can do is make your requests known. Don't passive-aggressively fix things to fit your wants. Just make your request so that the staff knows to expect it.

Sometimes it was as simple as "Mr. Smith likes to drive any cart he rides on, while Mr. Baker doesn't care if he drives or is the passenger -- so make sure you put Mr. Smith's bag on the driver's side". Not that it would be the end of the world if it was reversed, but then Mr. Smith would either have to swap bags himself or call a member of the staff over to fix the problem. The staff member swapping bags likely has better things to do (not that Smith is wrong to ask for it, more that the staff would have gotten it right the first time if they knew) and I've literally seen this scenario take the absolute worst turn it could. Mr. Smith forgot to fully clip Mr. Bakers's bag in, so as they drove away, Baker's bag went crashing down on the cart path sidewalk, either breaking or scuffing up a club or the golf bag. And it's not like we could point the finger and say Smith did it.

My favorite request was a member who always asked for a trio of cart towels to be "as wet you as you could get them." It was a weird request, but after the third or fourth time that he made that request, it dawned on me that this wasn't some fad that was going to go away and I embraced it. He was a good guy, so it wasn't hard to adapt. If I was on the opening squad and saw his name on the tee sheet, I'd grab three towels, toss them in the bottom of one of the twenty empty buckets sitting around in the cart barn, and fill the bucket with water. Hosing a towel down with a hose can get it wet, but letting it soak in a few gallons of water for three hours ensured that he got what he wanted. I made a point to keep an eye out for his arrival and would slop the towels on the panel just above the driver's side rear tire when he was in the golf shop, checking in. The first time I did it, the look of shock on the man's face was priceless. He was a ferocious courtroom litigator and senior/managing partner of his law firm, but in that moment, his face could have been that of a pre-school teacher. After I did it a few times, he once caught me in the staging area, and looked right at me. "You did this, right? I mean, you are the one who does this for me?"

I was a little embarrassed. It wasn't like I was saving the world, but I told him that I did.

"It doesn't happen when you aren't here. Thank you."

He shook my hand and went on his way up to the range. That's when I started making sure everyone knew to keep an eye out for his name on the tee sheet. By being a good guy, I was more than happy to spend the better part of seven seconds helping him out. The fact that he made a point to mention that he genuinely appreciated it, made it that much more likely to keep happening. If he was a dick about it, he would have had to ask every single time. And whomever was around, would probably take a random towel and dunk it in the dirtiest, stinkiest water they could find, fighting the urge to add to the water supply, in whatever manner they could manage. Hey. Get your head out of the gutter. The water in the ball washer is exponentially nastier than urine.

One way to make known how little you think of the staff, is to make it a point to hit golf balls at the guy driving the picker on the range. Yes, it's shielded. No, it's not perfect. Balls can get through, and what's more, any ball that hits the shielding makes an awful noise for whoever is inside. Accidental hits happen and nobody is going to get angry about that. If you are the golfer that hits the cart every time you are on the range, or you are always putting balls right around the picker (and yes, it's very easy to figure out where a ball came from) you are going to get a less than stellar reputation. One member in Flagstaff was a nice normal guy away from the range (or on a driving range that didn't have a picker driving around it). But as soon as the picker came onto the range, he'd turn into a hyperactive eight-year-old and just rapid fire as many balls as he could at the cart. He wasn't even taking full swings or setting his feet. I'd been the kid in the picker before when he did that -- which meant that I would spend all of my time picking up balls as far away from him as I could. I'd also been the assistant pro who felt compelled to tell a man nearly triple my age to grow up and stop being a dick to the twenty-year-old kid driving the picker.

One more thing on tipping that is somewhat commonplace. If you tell your buddy Jim that you are going to tip the guys on both yours and his behalf, you should make it a sizable tip. Nothing like the guy who normally throws a ten or twenty putting his wallet away after being told "Nah, Jim, I got the guys" and then you throw "the guys" two bucks. Half the time, Jim saw exactly what you did and would covertly slip someone his normal tip -- so now he and the staff both think you're a putz. Not a good look.

One last last thing, and I wish that this could go without saying, but I've seen it enough firsthand enough to include it for the few of you who still do this. Cheesy pickup lines delivered to the woman driving the beverage cart will not increase your chances of anything. Except maybe being made fun of by all those in ear shot and perhaps the rest of the employees when she gets back to the clubhouse and relays what stupid thing the guy in the red-striped shirt in the 10:30 group said. If you spent your formative years watching the first three minutes of a porn and you constantly wonder why the pizza delivery girl in real life never wants to come inside and personally inspect your sausage, then that's a *you* problem. In the history of attractive female beverage cart drivers, there's never been one that heard a terrible and borderline offensive line and thought "Well, that's someone I'd like to spend more time with in virtually any setting." Be better than that.

The Little Things So Many Golfers Miss

Golf is a popular sport but with that comes a mountain of misconceptions. There is a vast number of things that golfers assume about the game (or some part of the swing) that are misguided or just plain wrong. This is my attempt to tip the scales in the right direction.

There is no shortage of golfers who claim that the golf swing is this strange, convoluted contortion of the body that somehow ends up looking graceful if done right. This couldn't be further from the truth. A good golf swing is simple, because simple makes it easy to replicate -- and a good golf swing is nothing if you can't do it again and again. If you have to lift your front heel (left heel for righties, right heel for you lefties) to complete your backswing, you are likely taking your backswing too far. Not everyone should be John Daly. Hell, there's an argument that John Daly shouldn't be John Daly, but that's beside the point. A bad backswing puts you out of position, and if you are out of position it is very likely your swing will suffer. Short, simple backswings might lead to a little less distance, but a lot more consistency.

While we are on the topic of the swing, most people tragically misinterpret the wrist hinge or the way the wrist cocks. Your wrists do hinge and unhinge, as a way to generate extra speed. What they don't do, is wave back and forth as much as they hinge up and down. Picture a fisherman's casting motion for the wrist and you have the right idea -- or even a carpenter using a hammer. That whipping motion creates more club head speed, which is why you unhinge at the point of impact. Even if you don't think that you are hinging and unhinging your wrists, you are. Just keep in mind that, when you waggle a club back and forth before your swing, that isn't how your wrists will act when you actually make your swing.

Simplification doesn't just apply to your full swing. Every element of the golf game should be done as simply as possible. Don't overthink your shot selection. If you have one-fifty yards to the stick and you have a one-fifty club, just hit it. Don't take one extra club and swing easy, or one less club and over-swing. If you are playing in massive wind, take an extra club or two, but also keep in mind that a headwind (which means you are hitting into the wind) will hurt you far more than a tailwind (wind going with you) will help you. It ain't fair, but I'm not in charge of physics.

If your natural trajectory makes you hit a very high ball, don't take just one extra club in the wind -- take at least two, or maybe even three extra clubs. The wind is going to hurt you more. Granted, that means that if the wind dies, you are hosed and you will airmail the ball over the green. The alternative is to develop a punch shot, and that's now your wind play. Don't feel too bad. As you know, your high ball flight makes your iron shots stop pretty quickly when it isn't windy -- so you get a benefit on calm days. Golf's inherently a fair game, and there's no such thing as the best way to do things. Everything is a give and take.

Which is why the chip shot isn't necessarily better than a pitch shot, but you should figure out which one of them is your go-to around the green. You don't get a flow chart out there and even if you did, I can come up with a dozen instances where either one would work out. Don't vapor lock yourself on the side of the seventh green. Think of one of those two shots as your primary play and all things being equal, that's what you are going to do.

When you hit the green with your approach shot, you

likely left some sort of ball mark or divot (depending on what part of the country you are from, what it's called can change -- but it's not the beaver pelt of grass you took with your swing, it's the blemish your ball made on the green) and you need to fix it and fix it the right way. Which means using your divot repair tool (or in a pinch, you can use a tee) by sticking it in the green, and lifting it up until it's about level, then tamping it down with your putter.

Right?

Wrong.

When you pulled up on the grass, you likely did root damage. It won't show for a few days, or even a week, but you just made a bad situation worse.

Instead, you should use the tool and go around the edge of the divot, pushing grass into the center, then tamping it down. So why does everyone seem to do it wrong?

TV, is what everyone I've ever asked tells me. Tour pros do it the wrong way, everyone sees them and emulates it (though hopefully we all stop emulating Tour Pros soon). A few greenskeepers I've worked with, swear that the Tour Pro way of doing it is a good short-term solution. But that fixing divots the right way is a long-term fix and in the short-term still leaves a bit of a pockmark -- and the guys on Tour are far more pre-occupied with how the greens are going to look tomorrow and the next day, than they are in two weeks when they are a thousand miles away.

I get it and I'm not trying to paint them as monsters -- but they have to prioritize something and, all things being equal, most people will prioritize their own needs.

I banged this drum pretty hard earlier in the book, but I'm going to do it again, because it's so often badly done. When you are on the range, place your ball at the back edge of your previous divot. Save as much grass as possible for all future swings, including your own. Learn how to pick the right stall for your swing type (slicers head to the right and aim left, purveyors of the hook should set up shop on the left end and aim to the right) and truly -- never bang the same club mindlessly for twenty minutes at a time. Practice with a purpose and every swing should have a target.

When dealing with rangers, there are two common conversations that people have on the golf course. The first is "Why the hell is everything going so slowly in front of me and what are you going to do about it?" The second is "What? Me? I'm not the slow group, I've been waiting all day!" from the group who hasn't seen a group ahead of them for the last two hours.

Neither one is a good look on you. Trust me, if play in front of you has been slow, the ranger knows it. He just drove through it. And he likely knows exactly why it is that way. And, ten minutes before you copped an attitude with him, he was explaining to the offending party that they are messing up everyone's day. Sadly, that's kind of where it all ends. Unless you feel like the ranger is sitting on time travel capabilities and he just doesn't feel like sharing with the rest of us, there's nothing else he can do. If groups are stacked up, one after another, even if the slow group plays the next five holes at a record pace, there's still going to be a backup. There will probably be a backup for two hours after the slow group finishes. It's like freeway traffic, where everything suddenly goes down to two miles per hour, then you pass a bit of glass and metal debris and traffic picks up again.

No, there's not an accident to gawk at, but there was -- more than four hours ago. But there hasn't been a gap in people to let the backlog work itself out, so the ghost of an accident slows down traffic like the ghost of a slow group slows down the course. Which is why, when the ranger tells you that you are out of position and you need to speed up, even on the third or fourth hole, don't explain to him why he's wrong. You are doing everything in your power to mess up the golf course and everyone else's experience (or at least, the folks behind you), and he's going to have to deal with that hours after you've gone home. So, when the ranger says chop chop, the very least you can do is bite your tongue and grin -- when he drives away you should really find a reason to move with more purpose than you had a minute ago. You aren't a bad person. Just a slow one.

My very last point -- always be aware of your surroundings. As cell phones have become more prevalent and common courtesy has decreased (those two things may or may not be related, I'm not in a position to say with any certainty) we find ourselves creating noise and saying things that travel far beyond our sphere of influence. Golf courses haven't been explicitly designed to let you operate in your own little bubble, where you can call out whatever you want, whenever you want, without possibly interrupting someone else's conversation or backswing. The plot for *Outside Service* (which is about several guys working at golf course who start blackmailing the membership) was born as an idea roughly fifteen years before I actually started writing it. It popped in there because a member in Flagstaff started loudly describing the intimate relations he had with his wife, the moment their adult children left after staying with them for the weekend. He was telling his buddy, who was a few spots down on the range, but I was standing less than seven feet from him, cleaning his freshly used sand wedge. I wasn't being duplicitous. I wasn't crouched behind something to get the dirt. I'm pretty sure it was a Saturday, so the staff shirt was also bright red. Bright red shirt, nearly six feet tall and two-hundred and something pounds -- I was tough to miss. Only after he finished his story, did he realize that there was no scenario that could have kept me from hearing every detail he had announced. He then apologized with a face deeper red than my shirt.

I've said, or written, multiple times that working in golf is a lot like being one of Peter Pan's Lost Boys. And I'd worked in NeverNeverLand long enough to be anything but offended by this member's story, but it opened my eyes to how many people don't pay attention to what they are saying or doing, or where they are saying or doing it.

Don't be that guy on the golf course. Don't call out to your buddy Schmitty, who's up on the range, as you are walking out of the golf shop, because Mr. Baker is in the middle of his backswing on the adjacent fifth tee. Common courtesy is becoming far less common, but it doesn't have to be. Golf is a unique game, where we call penalties on ourselves and hold ourselves to a higher standard. That doesn't mean that we should exclude or shun those who don't act the part from playing this great game as much as it means that, as golfers, we should set a better example.

There are many things about golf that are strange. There's usually a reason why. For example:

If you are thinking of joining a club, see if they offer different levels of member, or membership packages. Pay close attention to what each membership entails. Some clubs allow all members make a tee time the same days in advance, while other clubs give preferential treatment for certain membership levels. So the highest paying members can make a time up to seven days in advance, while the lowest level only allows members to schedule a tee time three days out (keep in mind that you don't *have* to make then seven days out, just that you get first dibs at an empty tee sheet), and that can be problematic. Even if you aren't big on planning, when others have free reign with the tee sheet days before you, that means there is a good chance that you will rarely to get play when you want to. Which kind of sucks if you are a member of a course.

Daily fee courses prices fluctuate, but that doesn't mean that you should try to haggle on a cost. I mean, you are more than welcome to, but unless it's a small course (by that I meant the management company that actually runs the place), it's not going to happen.

If you hear that a course is suddenly very cheap, then you should be wary. Many good courses (perhaps all -- I hope all) aerate their greens, which means that they punch a ton of holes into their greens. This allows for a number of things that I don't quite understand (and you likely don't care about) but the final result is healthier greens. Unfortunately, for a little while, somewhere from a couple weeks to a month, it will be a genuinely bad experience to play that course.

Most of the people that run golf courses know this, and they plan ahead, to make sure it happens at the most opportune time for them. But golf courses do enjoy making money, so if a course with $250 greens fees suddenly starts charging far less, expect some punched greens. Depending on how punched the greens still are, you may be able to putt. Or it may be like sending a ball across a horizontal Plinko game. If it's the latter, so be it. You are getting to play a great course at a fraction of the cost. It won't work for your handicap or for your standard bet, but just pick it up on the green and add one or two, depending on how far out you are.

It's good to know that pertinent detail ahead of time though, so if you find a killer deal, it's probably worth calling the golf shop ahead of time and finding out if the greens were recently punched.

Getting out of the cart and walking a couple rounds a year isn't the worst thing ever. First, if you are out of shape, it will remind you how easy you normally have it and you'll appreciate your normal rounds more. Secondly -- and more importantly -- you may find that it allows you to focus on your game more. Since you have to move quickly in order to keep pace, you will find that you move more purposefully toward your ball. The solitude of walking will allow you time to analyze your shot as you walk up the fairway to the green.

If you'd like to know how to pick the proper set of tees, it is remarkably easy. Look over the scorecard, specifically looking for the length of the par-fours. If your group has no hope of getting to each one in two (that is, after a tee shot and an approach you should be on the green -- and ideally not driver/driver or driver/three-wood) then you may want to move up a tee box. The premise of par for a certain hole is how many shots it should take (which is calculated as however many full swings it should take you to get on the green, then add two putts). A par-three should take one swing and then two putts. A par-four should be two swings followed by two putts. If that isn't feasible, then set yourself up to win and change tee boxes. Not to say that it needs to be 100% accessible (having one long and punishing par-four isn't a big deal). But knowing that most golf course layouts have at least ten par-fours, some as many as fourteen -- the vast majority of holes should be in play. Swallow your pride, move up a box and enjoy the game more.

On that note, stop comparing yourself to other players. You do not know their life story and they do not know yours. Trying to hit it further than the guy a few over on the driving range isn't a good use of your time. Play your game and remember that it may be in your competitor's best interest to try to rope you into playing his game. If a guy is shit talking what you are doing on the course, it probably means what you are doing is working. Play your game.

Jeff Beck

Fun fact -- if you hit a hole-in-one and don't tell every person you meet for the next four years, they say you haven't actually hit a hole-in-one.

Unfortunately, the previous fact is false. You really don't need to make it your new thing. Before you were the guy who liked golf, now you're the guy that likes to talk about his hole-in-one. Here's the thing about holes-in-one: they are 100% luck. No one has the ability to hit a golf ball exactly where they want to, in a 4.25" hole, from one to two hundred yards away. Yes, ability can make it so that you are in the general vicinity or even within a ten-foot radius around the cup. Anything that happens after that is pure luck. Strangely enough, some people seem to get luckier than others (not counting the former dictator in North Korea, who claimed he got at least one, but perhaps as many as four holes-in-one every time he teed it), and I have no explanation why. Just keep playing, and firing at the stick, and maybe it'll happen for you.

This might sound strange or counterintuitive, but bear with me. The employees at your golf course have no idea what the weather is going to do by the minute. They can tell you what frequently happens when this kind of storm moves in, but they have absolutely no idea when you will be able to resume your round.

SUCK LESS AT GOLF

However, it is in your best interest to listen to them when weather can be dangerous. More and more golf courses are equipped with lighting detection hardware that gives an accurate readout of what is happening, in regards to the electricity in the air.

First, we get it. You didn't want to come in. You wanted to finish. You were very close, now you have to wait around and your day is getting longer by the second. Trust me, we get it. That said, we're dealing with electricity here. Little known fact, lightning is incredibly dangerous and can move very quickly. This round of golf, or more accurately, wrapping up this round of golf in a timely manner isn't nearly as important as your life.

I've seen a few pictures of the aftermath when someone is hit by lightning. Being struck by lightning happens more often than you would think, likely because each and every one of us is toting around a collection travel-sized lightning rods. On occasion we even hold one of them above our heads, making them that much more attractive to the giant bolts of lightning. Lightning carries an insane amount of energy, and when struck, it runs through the body. Everything explodes. The metal and graphite in golf clubs peel apart, and the human body reacts similarly. Few live through the experience, and the ones who do have their lives change in many ways.

But sure, let's focus some more about how much better things would have been if you only had another fifteen or twenty minutes to finish.

As someone who has counseled hundreds of concerned golfers during rain delays, just relax. No one has any idea what's going to happen, or when it's going to happen. Just grab a drink (maybe not a cocktail but I'm firmly on team No Judgment) and try to remember that you are doing something that most other people aren't doing on that day. Most people in this country would happily swap days with you versus whatever they're doing.

If it's only raining, and there's no lightning around, you should finish. It is only water and you'll dry off. And it doesn't matter if you've spent time around the Oregon coast (where they golf pretty much no matter what) and the rain doesn't bug you or if you are on the opposite end of the spectrum and see rain once a decade, because then it's something new to experience. Rain is to be played through and in and lightning is to be run from as fast as humanly possible.

Some final thoughts to leave you with:

Be realistic about your own game. Play fast. Replace your divots. Get lessons sporadically. Give your clubs time to mature and learn how to truly use them. Spend most of your time on your short game. Learn how to hit the ball hard enough so it dies at the cup. Find a golfing friend. Let the faster group play through. Walk at least one round per year. Smile at the kid scrubbing your clubs, and throw him a five or more. Shorten your backswing. Swear to never use the phrase "grip it and rip it" or to be the guy in a gallery who screams "it's in the hole!" every time your golfer of choice tees off. Watch more of the LPGA and learn whatever you can from them. Play the numbers and take the smart route. Stop looking at your scorecard so closely and just play the game.

It's a damn good one.

Author's Note

Well, there it is. That's the distillation of most of my golf knowledge. People who know me can attest that this is the abridged version -- I could have done a full chapter on checking lies of your irons or advanced putting theory. You got the toned-down version of my "slow play is killing golf" sermon. If buy me a beer or seven, you can get the full-strength dose. It ain't pretty.

A lot of this book is common sense, though some of it flies in the face of logic. I stand behind it. If there's something you don't agree with, you are more than welcome to ignore it. We can disagree and still be civil. If you'd like some clarification or you are dead set that I am very wrong, feel free to send me an email and let's talk.

Never lose track of the fact that golf is supposed to be fun and if you aren't enjoying it, you may need to take a step back. Short breaks, or even long ones, have led to people enjoying the game far more. Golf is bigger than any of us and you can break yourself upon it.

SUCK LESS AT GOLF

I'd like to take a moment and thank my many golf mentors. Jim Davison, Matt Bailey, Jason Bangild, Eric Slack, Jeff Ulvedal, Todd Cernohaus, Brock Weiss, Molly Sutherland, Reuben Vigeuroa, Jim Saunders, Hank Gardner, and Steve Dahlby taught me more about the game and the business of golf than I could have imagined there was there to learn. Being years removed from the industry hasn't jaded me or fused rose-colored lenses over my eyes, but the years I spent working with all you were amazing. So many stupid anecdotes and inside jokes came to mind as I was combing through my memory -- thanks guys.

A huge thanks to Todd, Big Matt, Hickle, Nelly, and literally at least two hundred more guys and gals that I worked with.

If you enjoyed this book, or learned anything from it, I'd love to hear from you. I'd greatly appreciate a review on Amazon. If this book found its way to you, then odds are good you would appreciate my first novel, *Outside Service*, the one about the employees blackmailing the members. You might enjoy my follow-up novel, *Prove Me Wrong*, as well. Though it has very little to do with golf -- but I think it's still a good story.

Thanks for reading, and I genuinely hope this book

has helped your game in some way. Find *your* pro and go get a lesson. Just not too many of them -- four lessons a week is way too many.

Unless you are tackling the flop shot. In that case, you might want to sign up for two-a-days.

Jeff Beck
5/29/17

About the Author

Jeff Beck lives with his wife, Stephanie, and their daughter Emma. A Phoenix native, he graduated from Northern Arizona University with a BS in Journalism. His novels include *Outside Service* and *Prove Me Wrong*, in addition to the non-fiction *Suck Less At Golf*.

Photograph by Stephanie Beck.

Made in the USA
Lexington, KY
24 January 2018